# Pearl

## Poems by Tom Murphy

www.flowersongpress.com

FLOWERSONG
PRESS

FlowerSong Press
McAllen, Texas 78501

Copyright © 2020 by Thomas Michael Murphy

ISBN: 978-1-7345617-0-8

Published by FlowerSong Books
in the United States of America.
www.flowersongpress.com

Set in Adobe Garamond Pro

Cover art by Jimmy Peña
Photograph by Mot
Typeset and graphic design by Matthew Revert

No part of this book may be reproduced without
written permission from the publisher.

All inquiries and permission requests should be
addressed to the Publisher.

2nd Edition

## Previously Published Poems
## A warm gratitude to all the editors for publishing these works:

*Ain't Gonna Be Treated This Way: Celebrating Woody Guthrie, Poems of Protest & Resistance*
"The American Axiology of Guns"

*Birth of Tragedy* "Colma"

*Boundless Anthology* "Dawn Moist"

*Box of Words* "Someone Once Told Me as a Boy"

*Chupacabra Anthology* "Chupacabra and Welder Mask Man"

*Corpus Christi Writers 2018: An Anthology* "Obituary (*Muwashshaha*)," "Richard Brautigan's Other Suicide," "Then Again, On the Road," and "You Tender Hogs"

*Corpus Christi Writers 2019: An Anthology* "Warp and Woof"

*Illya's Honey* "Corpus Sunrise," and "West Texas Desert Bloom"

*Langdon Review* (2016) "Chaos," "Guernica Gernika," "Her Crossed Legs Show," "Lichgate," "Ms. Lila Tomczak," "Prometheus Unbound," "Sonnet I," and "Written Robes,"

*Nothing Journal* "The Last Woman on the Earth"

*Poets Responding to SB 1070* "Sacred Water (*Muwashshaha*)"

Red River Review "27 Julio 2015," "7 13 15 (Campo Grande)," "The Death of Jocelyn Jones," "I am Werg," "Kiss the Boot," and "Sallipraxius"

*SCMLA 2019* Winter Newsletter "Fall"

*Speak Your Mind: Woody Guthrie Poets, Celebrate Freedom of Speech 2019, Poems of Protest & Resistance* "Protest Infinity," and "Wedding Dress"

*Spirit Makes Life* "Thinking of You, Robb Jackson"

*Stone Renga* "Moon Earth Eros Sun"

*Stories and Poems from Close to Home* "April," and "Fun with Sound"

*Switchgrass Review* "The Last Days of Cherry"

*Voices de la Luna* "You Want to Bring Your Guns to My Class"

*Writing Texas* "Ibn Zayún to Wallada," and "Perfume Breeze"

**Explanatory Notes and Acknowledgements**

The Barron Park *Diwan*\* poems came from having grown up in this unincorporated California neighborhood surrounded by Palo Alto (1965-1975). In 1975, the Barron Park Association voted to join Palo Alto, primarily for the fire and police support. There were stipulations associated with this change, though. Sidewalks were not required; although Barron Park had some, many of its streets had none. Soon after the vote, all the massage parlors and the strip joint in south Palo Alto were shuttered. My Barron Park poems are for those who lived in Barron Park before it became part of Palo Alto. They might be surprised to know that today their former neighborhood is made up of multi-million-dollar homes, with most of the old ones either razed or rebuilt to suit. Some of these readers may be unhappy with both what is said and what is left unsaid.

To the following people I dedicate this section: Alan and Chas Murphy, Jim Jacobsen, John Chovanec, Todd Taylor, Pearl Krause, Members of Troop 54, Scott Fessenden, and Vietnam veteran Jerrold Louis Vesey (November 29, 1949-August 25, 1970).

The Lichgate *Diwan* poems do not occur out of the blue. Many people who have helped, encouraged, encountered and guided. The Spain poems especially involved: David Blanke, Janet Blanke, Marybeth Davis, Pam Meyers, Don Luna, Javier Villarreal, Leticia Villarreal, Carrie Mae Pierce, Jeff Grimes, Chelsie Hawkinson, Melissa Culver, Joe Jozwiak, Susan Wolff Murphy, Juan Carlos y Elena of *El Espectacular* and my students. On the home front, I wish to thank: Alan Berecka, Robin Carstensen, Stefan Sencerz, Juan Manuel Pérez, Malia Pérez, Chuck Etheridge, John "One Deep" Meza, Odilia Galván Rodríguez, Bill Mays, Mike Linaweaver and Friends of Padre. With a special thanks to Pam Brouillard and Glenn Blalock. I also wish to thank my writer friends: Carol Coffee Reposa, Larry "Buffalo" Thomas, Michelle Harmon, Jeanetta Calhoun Mish, Edward Vidaurre of FlowerSong Books, Nathan Brown, PW Covington, Dorothy Alexander, Ken Hada, Katie Hoerth, Hank Jones, Julie Chappell, Paul Juhasz, Ann Howells, Charlotte Renk, Ron Wallace, Bill Grasso, Terry Dalrymple, Andrew Geyer, Lyman Grant, Mik Parent, Paul Austin, Octavio Quintanilla, Floyd Salas, Claire Ortalda, Gillian Conoley, Marilyn Robitaille and Moumin Quazi. Finally, I wish to thank those associated with Black Mountain College: Brian Butler, Alice Sebrell, Jeff Davis, Hilary Holladay and Ted Pope.

For my daughters Sophia, Anna, & Elanor<br>Especially for Susan

* *Diwan* "Arabic word for 'a gathering, a collection or anthology' of poems" from *Poems for the Millennium: The University of California Book of North African Literature*, Vol. 4, page 2. Pierre Joris and Habib Tengour editors.

## *Barron Park Diwan*

| | |
|---|---|
| 15 | Fun with Sound |
| 16 | Prometheus Unbound |
| 18 | Wandering the Seasons of Bol Park |
| 21 | Someone Once Told Me as a Boy |
| 22 | Ms. Lila Tomczak |
| 24 | April |
| 26 | Colma |
| 28 | Upon News |
| 30 | In Memoriam Lisa Borrall Evans Brown |
| 32 | Sonnet I |
| 33 | These Salons of Ours |
| 36 | Ashtrays |
| 38 | Civic Center BART Station |
| 40 | Pearl |
| 46 | Caught in the Nick of Naked Time |
| 47 | Looking Away for all the Wrong Reasons image |
| 48 | Frogs Are Easy to Find |
| 50 | What People Wanted Me to Do |
| 51 | Rocks |
| 52 | Barron Park Image |
| 53 | Brain Tumors of Barron Park |
| 55 | Steve Wilhite |
| 56 | Fifth of November |
| 57 | Your Barron Park |
| 61 | Not Weird Enough |
| 62 | If You Took Anything from Berkeley |
| 64 | Graham Thomas *Lonicera Periclymenum* |

| | |
|---|---|
| 65 | The Transitory Troika |
| 66 | Lower Barron |
| 68 | I Know the Day I'll Die |
| 69 | Ruggles and Bukowski |
| 73 | Wong Manor |
| 74 | The Cockroach's Worth |
| 76 | Secrets and Lies: Father's Confessions |
| 79 | Kiss the Boot |
| 80 | Halloween |
| 84 | Brother Pneumonia |
| 86 | Too Much a California Boy |
| 87 | Rebuke |
| 89 | Terry Martin |

## *Lichgate Diwan*

| | |
|---|---|
| 101 | The Last Days of Cherry |
| 107 | That Asteroid |
| 108 | Guernica Gernika |
| 110 | The Last Woman on Earth |
| 111 | Lichgate |
| 113 | Corpus Sunrise |
| 114 | 7 13 15 (Campo Grande) |
| 115 | Savio's Rubric |
| 118 | Perfume Breeze |
| 119 | The Last Time I Was in Paris |
| 120 | ¡Ya Basta! |
| 121 | Hair |
| 123 | Dawn Moist |

| | |
|---|---|
| 124 | The Swagman's Bag |
| 125 | The Death of Jocelyn Jones |
| 127 | Who Can Forgive and Forget |
| 128 | Sonnet II |
| 129 | Naked Panama Nights |
| 130 | Lost Song of Pilar (*Canción perdida de Pilar*) |
| 132 | The American Axiology of Guns |
| 133 | I Am Eros |
| 134 | Wedding Dress |
| 136 | Sacred Water |
| 139 | Richard Brautigan's Other Suicide |
| 140 | 27 Julio 2015 |
| 142 | Scofflaw and Squander |
| 144 | Ibn Zaydún to Wallada |
| 145 | Invocation |
| 147 | Thinking of You, Robb Jackson |
| 149 | Pairs, Thrice |
| 151 | My Whisper |
| 152 | Death Stairs |
| 154 | On Each Other's Birthday |
| 156 | The Divisionist |
| 157 | Chupacabra and Welder Mask Man |
| 158 | After the Hurricane |
| 160 | Her Crossed Legs Show |
| 161 | Written Robes |
| 162 | The Mathematics of the Last Act |
| 163 | Obituary |
| 165 | Sallipraxius |
| 166 | Update |

| | |
|---|---|
| 167 | 7 18 16 |
| 171 | Ofay |
| 172 | Song Poem Wha be Wha |
| 175 | Chaos |
| 177 | Protest Infinity Pantoum |
| 179 | West Texas Desert Bloom |
| 180 | You Tender Hogs |
| 182 | Hand Written Language Analysis |
| 183 | I Am Werg |
| 184 | Still Life |
| 185 | Then Again, On the Road |
| 186 | Warp and Woof |
| 201 | You Want to Bring Your Guns to My Class |
| 202 | Moon Earth Eros Sun |
| 204 | Fall |

*Glossary*

**Aumakua** Hawai'ian family deity typified as either a shark or an owl

**Bolgia** evil ditches in Dante's *Inferno*

**eguzki** Basque, meaning 'sun'

**farkle** Pop culture word, meaning 'wimp out'

**Hale o Kapuni heiau** Hawai'ian Shark Temple on the island of Hawai'i

**Ibn Zaydún** 11th century poet of the Caliphate of Córdoba, lover of Wallada

**Kaaipai** Hawi'ian shark deity

**Mailekini** Shark Temple sitting stone

**MDC** (Millions of Dead Cops) punk band whose song "John Wayne Was a Nazi" was popular

**Muwashshaha** al Andalusian indigenous poetic form

**Ogbanje iyi-uwa** Ibo phrase, a changeling (ogbanje) represented by a special stone (iyi-uwa) that forms the link between real and spirit world—stone needs to be found to destroy changeling

**Pu' u Kohalā** Hill of the Whale at the Hawi'ian Shark Temple

**Uukanipo** Hawi'ian shark twin deities

**Wallada bint al-Mustakfi** 11th century poet of the Caliphate of Córdoba, lover of Ibn

*Was that you bound in sun on the step, living the life of the seasons, and loving*

> From "It was the Beginning of Joy and the End of Pain"
> by Gillian Conoley

*When you come, bring me a tourniquet for our wounded moon*

> From "Song of the Broken Giraffe" by Bob Kaufman

Barron Park, 1948

# Barron Park *Diwan*

# Fun with Sound

I carry my hatchet around with me.
It lies under my bed when I sleep.

I listen to music in my room
and freak out with my hatchet
pretending to smash the furnishings
trashing the air
to the beat.

No one has ever seen me
when I freak in my room.

Come over sometime.

# **Prometheus Unbound** (for Corey Larson)

Zitkála-Ša dragged
from under a bed,

kicking and punching,
into the light. Bound

tight to a chair; rope-burn.
One by one, her braids cut

transformed into a coward.
Lost more than her religion

as her whole being swayed
off kilter in cold Dakota.


Like Zitkála-Ša,
I was tied to a chair

hair too short to shear, then.
Crime—standing at school desk,

to write as I do now. Vertical.
to write this poem; upright

on feet. Too much energy
to sit still. All of my life

except episodes of depression
depths of profound drunkenness.


My binder, Mr. Godseye,
6th grade teacher, other students

the laugh track. Those dead
voices spread the cold snow

of Dakota throughout
my brainpan. Pelos long,

my rebellious nature has
mashed Zitkála-Ša's turnips

until the jar's bottom broke
clean free and fell; unbound.

# Wandering the Seasons of Bol Park

Barbed wire kept out the kids
                         most of the time.
But there were paths
                   near the creek
through the middle of the field
and along the old railroad track.

The dilapidated barn
nestled in tow straw
                windblown

I went through it once—
disheveled torn blankets
on a dirt floor

dried timbers on the outskirts
of lawless Barron Park
                beckoned fire.
It burned one night

before the Barron Park Association
bought the land to make Bol Park
Before Barron Park voted in '75
to join *perfect* Palo Alto.

Mr. Ken Arutunian gave his time
to make Bol Park our neighborhood gem

with Eagle Scout projects
planting live oaks, redwoods,
tearing the burnt barn down for safety.

May fete and pancake breakfasts
under oak boughs on rolling grass.
The back quarter wild
like the old neighborhood itself.

                    A gravel crunch
dried leaves crackle
and the dingle ball size
redwood pinecones
underfoot, tramping
in and out the shade
of oak boughs, summer swelter
even within fifty feet of cool
Matedero Creek.

Green rolling grass leads
to tall dun that hides
an old rusting reaper.

PA paved the old railroad line,
a bike path that connects
Stanford land—not everybody
cared for the farm or PA.

Now, Palo Alto demands
a Bol Park bike park—
rip out the oaks and rural
setting a neighborhood

has loved since it bought
the land for the park—.
Adding a toilet for visitors.
Get your own damn park!

Bol Park is Barron Park's.
Palo Alto politics
                       idiocy and inane,
wandering the seasons of Bol Park

Acacias blooming in February
in a dazzling array of yellow
against fresh green leaves.

Somewhere on the sunken
railroad line that cut through
smokers' hill years ago—
                       I found the spike
that's on my poetry bookshelf.

Let not a planning commission
destroy our nurtured earth
that holds a community together.
Leave Bol Park au natural.

# Someone Once Told Me as a Boy

Someone once told me as a boy
There are partitions in my mind
Search and destroy

Be filled with fear, have no joy
Blackness overtakes the heart in time
Someone once told me as a boy

Break car windows to enjoy
Steal all the money you can find
Search and destroy

Watch out for the smiling ploy!
Rip you off is on their mind
Someone once told me as a boy

Spotlight pigs arrive to annoy
Casual enough to skip the bind
Search and destroy

Trabajo en la noche me voy
All for me and none of your kind
Someone once told me as a boy
Search and destroy

## Ms. Lila Tomczak

                    Ms. Lila Tomczak,
Greek myth introducer, poem promoter,
story instigator in a word – lover of the word.
Tubers. But at All Hallows' Eve,

ire more than *bon mot*, the bent-down anarchist.
The leftover can of shaving cream
sprayed upon the seat behind the didactic tableaux.

"Damn you!" She would have said if she
knew. In Jackson's mother's voice,
from when Ms. Lila Tomczak read "The Lottery,"

"What? What is it?" Her hand on the chair back,
after helping one-on-one, face-to-face
a student. She pulled the chair out.

Scrutiny,
                the bodies lean forward,
grins smirk, smacking their chops. "What?"
She sat for a moment, "Oh my God!" Popped up

like flames through the roof.
                    The glance, then a
crab skitter – never allows her tormentors
a view before out the door. And the babble began

as also the sweat
                over the errant can of shaving cream
between inner sleeve and boyish,
hairless, under arm. Door flew open.

All agape. "Somebody has got to pay
for the dry cleaning. I mean it,"
Wiping the chair clean

with brown industrial paper towels.
"I don't want you to tell me here," dumps
the last foam into the brown trashcan. "Put a note

in my box."
                "Now," sat Ms. Lila Tomczak,
"discuss the descent of Persephone."

# April

Named for my month
I laugh in your face
Oh! Ah ha! Ah ha!

Heard your shrill voice
I remember your face
Hee hee! Hee hee!

Once, you readied for battle
before you came to class
Oh! Ha ha! Ah ha!

You couldn't sit still
had a bee up your ass
Ha ha!

I saw you today
you slimy thing
you said, "had one glass of wine
now I have a frazzled mind"
Ho ho! Hee hee!

You praised what I had done
said, "I had good feeling"
I smashed your face
after you called me a good being
La la! Ha ha!

Go see the play up the street
the one you said was so neat
Ah ha! Ho ho!

But don't come back when I'm mad
kick your face then I'll be glad
Ho ho! La la! Hee hee! Ha ha!

# Colma

Have you been to the city of Colma
where the living are outnumbered
by the dead?

Just cruise up El Camino de Real,
check out the ten-plus
graveyards
for Jews
gooks
wops
micks
even space for me
I suppose.

Look at the headstones
for sale
buy here
lie here
but why here?

What?
just around the hill
from San Francisco
can't stink up the city
with death.
Ha!

Remember

drink a six-pack

before

going to Colma

they're many stones

to piss on.

# Upon News

Trying to get my head straight after
traveling and finding out my friend

Tom Barry died from cirrhosis.
Ironic as it may be, many vocalized

that path was mine. Somehow
I managed to come to grips with

myself. The loss of his laughter hurts.
We were rather close for a good

ten years of debauchery; he was 46.
We were sardonic, sarcastic, and unsatisfied.

Silly as it may be, I'm still that way
sans the daily drunkenness and drugs.

The edge is purely a mental state of
rigid tautness that still perpetuates the

fight for breaths of life and a course
hardly lit; as to stumble upon the moment.

If it were only a blue daze or lobelia
strewn path, the battleship gray would flow

as fog that clings like mountain skirts
that swish by zephyr and there the girls run

unimpeded, their minds cut cleaner than
Ockham's razor stored under a glass pyramid.

Amidst the calligraphy of war stroked
in the tone of mango madness before the L.A.

cattle drive converges into a rumba tempo
over the grapevine where U-Haul Bob stalks

the pass for the stranded with the promise of
salvation, but it's known that white line dissipated.

An axiom per Blake on excess, the proof a
drowned tiki harbinger surrounded with 40s

in a tight group spread around the bent
steel frame bed. The death rattle wrung a clarion

like a claxon squeak of terror,
frail, bedraggled, then expelled.

# In Memoriam Lisa Borrall Evans Brown

Did she die on her birthday?
Was it self-inflicted or just a part of life?
Tough questions, but sexy Lisa is gone.

I remember her in her short skirt
dancing outfit twirling so her black panties
were for all to see, her blonde hair sway.

Only a freshman then, she was a dream
to my young eyes. Through FB, some 40 years later,
we connected again. When I stated I had kissed

Laura Grahms behind the couch in 3rd grade
Lisa's comment was, "You were a sexpot!"
She was deeply moved with the Klimt

nudes I messaged her on consecutive
birthdays. We were thousands of miles apart
in so many ways. Her husband's death

eight years ago, haunted her as viewed
through her memory posts online
though since January, her comments and likes

tapered off to almost nothing at all.
She used to upload pictures of her lovely garden
or fresh snow, or delicious meals, or her

loveable black lab Roo on walks.
Who will walk Roo now? What will her
children do with her Portland home? Where

did her heart finally fail to beat?
Her blonde hair gone silver though, she
commented how her and her friends' legs

were up in the air in cars parked in the hills
during their senior year. Lisa's drawn unicorn
next to her senior portrait with one word: Free

## Sonnet I

Dear daddy,
why can't we be remembered
as Priam and Pyrrhus
in Aeneas' tale to Dido
that Hamlet so fondly reminisces.
Or the care Bloom takes
when Daedalus sees Edward the Seventh
that *Absinthe Greeneyed monster* lurch

in Nighttown.                    Though it'll be
the Colonel calling me Benedict
with the caveat that I have
all the attributes of a dog
except loyalty;
that's how they'll remember us.

# These Salons of Ours

The whole garage—our domain.

Framed wood and black papered building

        open to the pitched roof

                on a hard concrete slab.

Uncovered these tools, dangerous without guards,

                belt and wheel of a table saw,

                      jagged blades tempered, rusting.


                              Here, we entertain.

The drawing room of animated minds

                pens, paper, pastels & canvas

among the scattered detritus of

        consumer crap in broken wrappers,

        boxes labeled *junk* stacked askew,

broken chairs heaped upon a threadbare couch,

clothes drying on a frayed line strung across the expanse,

stolen Colorado Highway 291 sign nailed to a split wood strut,

assorted saws, extension cords, hedge clippers and *the* hatchet.


Camera        shutter        clicks,

tape players,

    one blasts hardcore punk

        or industrial monotones,

            the other records the click click—clack clack,

                snort and banter.


We hung ourselves

    out 'n whet our appetite

        with beers and lines.

Drinking sessions start with exotic global exports,

       ending with cheapest 7-11 12-pack.

              All night cocaine bashes

                     in these salons

                            of ours.

# Ashtrays

Ashtrays were on every table in the family home on Barron.
The large ornate brown glass housed in a brass shell that
moved from coffee table to end tables in the living room.
At times overflowing with ash and crunched up Pall Mall stubs.

The culled small glass ashtrays from western National Park lodges
like the emblazed Thunderbird in clear glass from Bryce, Zion
and the North Rim. Or the pilfered brown glass Jackson Lake
Lodge with its silhouette logo of the Tetons below the butts.

The blue glass extracted from a dumpy Reno hotel
embedded the promise of glitz with sparkling stars that
scraped the master bath tub edge where my father sat on
the john reading his porn books for hours and smoking.

Or on the redwood table on the back porch where we ate
dinner summer eves sat the two abalone shells. And in the
really old days, there also sat a squat Almaden bottle, layers of
candle drips of multicolored wax down its green glass side.

In the kitchen, a rotisserie of ashtrays from counter to
table, the constant thin line of smoke ever rising, sometimes
the words verbalized, "hand me that ashtray, would you." The
rasp of glass on wood as it slid across the sheen into his grasp.

After a Pall Mall Red not fastened between tray spokes
unattended, tumbling down to gold carpet left to slowly burn

a two-inch mark below the IBM XT and Epson printer on
the long foldup table—finding that burn freaked him out.

In the master bedroom was hidden the sacred heavy brass tray—
a used artillery tube shell that had engraved around the wide lip
"U.S.S. Arizona Library"—snatched by Alan Campbell, a great
uncle's brother, who on the beachhead of Guadalcanal died.

Years later, Dad wrote a letter; I, suspicious of it being semi-nasty
from comments like, "This ashtray should not sit on some
fat-ass admiral's desk." The dot-matrix letter packaged up with
the reworked brass shell and mailed to the Honolulu Memorial.

All the ashtrays were put away and the chipped ones thrown out
when he found out he had inoperable lymphatic cancer next to
his heart and he quit his five pack a day habit, but too late, dying
thirteen months later after chemo and radiation at sixty-two.

All my ashtrays are gone, although we do have two rather large
clam shells plucked off the beach from the OBX on the patio
for guests. Once again, I find I must shed my semi-hid habit
before the impending emphysema or the big C pays dividends.

# Civic Center BART Station

The sun first struck the mesa at Acoma.
Cisterns full of fresh rainwater, like words
spoken, *we are not safe from fire here*,
that crystalline dawn lost the crisp air.

David Lynch says, Haley's Comet's come and gone.

San Francisco's Ferry Building clock spire disappears
bottom up at the end of Market Street with each
step taken down the broken escalator. Below
traffic weight, bay-fill jelly nestled, the faux
marble BART platform flat round seat, like
a sculpture dais, sits a younger man than I. He
quickly stands, barely out of reach. His rumpled
hair and clothes make it clear that he's not slept.

A portable mirror framed that
nervy blue eye stare with mahogany;
the entropy, his face is mine. His mouth opens
as a BART train zips electric tracks, bleeps
twice while the ionize breeze taps his forehead
with cock-a-doodle strands, my follicles
only skull peek as fresh grass pops
the earth-crust. His mute lips speak—

David Lynch says, Sam Clemens's born and Mark Twain dies in Haley's Comet years.

Long after one night's fidget tent bivouac
Adirondack forest—bear infested, sports page
and hatchet. Five miles down a dirt road,
so crooked, fringed with bushes.

Early morning dust trails the Winnebago
coat-hanger down the Corolla window
to deliver ignition key and mobility.
The whole country seems fluid to the eye.

David Lynch says, In 1809, Lincoln's born the exact moment as Charles Darwin.

Profusely *thanked* at campsite edge, a question
rises: "In that house of torture, hadn't he been able to
read, write, think, without being disturbed?"
The Winnebago's engine rumbles codified words,
"I hope you think now that all New Yorkers aren't assholes."
dog-leapt in wheel dust yelping, "I don't. I don't."

# Pearl

On this Friday as November turns towards winter, my thoughts gravitate towards you, Pearl, living in your rented white farm house next door. An easy walk through the hedge gap to your wisteria laden stoop with the McGovern for President bumper sticker on an upper beam. An oak desk inside the enclosed porch, then the step up over the worn wood threshold to the living room and another oak desk—they look toward each other through the glassless windows.

Pearl, once, I remember my brother Chas and I facing each other at the uneven desks—wood carved cats our totems as you, Pearl, sway as a wood stork with awkward feet between the living room bookshelves, chairs and a saggy green-gold couch to the bright white end of the country kitchen, where gnarled deft hands created scratch wedding cakes, vinegar catsup with tang zing.

Pearl, you shared a love of reading as books lined the walls from the scandalous Millers to Will and Ariel Durant's *The Story of Civilization*. On Saturdays, we all crossed the street to the Bookmobile. Later, Durant's volumes through *Rousseau and Revolution* adorned our wooden shelves.

Pearl, when the street crews tarred and graveled the rough roads throughout our humble Barron Park you persuaded the workers to dump a huge load of gravel to spread down your lengthy drive, where later parked the travel van the size of a UPS truck that slept ten. You would travel states with friends to mysterious locations, Pearl, stopping where you wished, settling for a night or more.

Pearl, as Bear the cat right now is on my desk so did your orange long haired cat you named Damnit sleep in the comfort of your warm home where Gordo the blind toy bulldog's nails scrape across the wooden floors following your heels through your many rooms.

Pearl, you liked bourbon straight in a highball glass and had a master's in English literature. Hitchhiked in your 20s during the Great Depression from your native home east across this wide hip country by yourself. How did you pay your way, Pearl? Although you married late to Oscar Krause, who took his life in your gravel drive while sitting in the car's front seat, a hose connected to the exhaust snaked up through the window for his eternal sleep, you never had kids, or grandkids but you treated us three boys as such. Pearl, in your always clicking mouth, your tongue rolled my name as a pebble that murmured Tommy.

You taught me that fallen golden apricots and purple plums could be dried, but Pearl, I couldn't eat the red figs you said were so tender. You were well liked by my great-grandmother Joah Norris, a reformed Quaker; you two would knit and visit together as she stayed over for a fortnight.

Pearl, I remember when you had Alan Larsen and Jim Hoffman clear out the backyard center. They laid out a gravel square, built a redwood frame with shelves topped by a slatted roof—a gazebo for your gardening passion when not in the kitchen. Pearl, you tended to your plants, a cornucopia of purple irises, fiery snapdragons, pansies, petunias, mums and tall stem zinnias. Color patches dotted the front and back yards like the wet palette of Monet's Giverny.

You were so kind to us boys, Pearl, allowing us space for permanent forts that were cobbled with fence scraps. My brothers on the backside of the old farm tool shed that was once a chicken coop and they had stolen wood platforms for the floor. Pearl, my fort with a steep slanting linoleum roof sat between the redwood fence and your white clapboard sides—a good place to hide from the rain, from my father or the Vietnam war on TV.

Pearl, you wore hand sewn black leather shoes for your problem feet that pedaled a three-wheel bike with a large wire basket behind the seat on the back over the wheels. Your transportation in Barron Park and beyond since you did not drive.

In May '67, after dad delivered the pinewood derby track and then the folks flew to London, Munich, Paris and DC—gone for over a month. Pearl, you took care of us boys, cooking our meals, getting us off to school, even putting me in the bike basket as we rode out of Barron Park to cross El Camino and then railroad tracks to Alma's far side where my nursery school teacher, Miss Wise, would meet us and then take me in her car to Menlo Park. I never felt too comfortable sitting in that basket, rather vulnerable, bouncing around in the metal mesh as you, Pearl, pedaled beyond six lanes of traffic and the railroad tracks; an animal on display.

At a young age, Pearl, I substituted for Alan's *San Francisco Chronicle* route—folding and tossing papers around Barron Park—I took over Chas' *Santa Clara Valley Journal* paper route—a three day a week thin periodical that diminished to once a week. Besides you, Pearl, few read that rag over the covered route of houses, apartments and the mobile home park behind All American Market.

Pearl, I never took it too seriously and only tried collecting the 40¢ per subscriber a few times throughout the neighborhood, stopping at the Grieshaber and Ida's and the black fellow all on Ilima Court. Or on the route with Jim once, we played basketball with papers at net-less hoop at the end of San Jude, leaving a few folded ones on that house roof before that ugly trouble at the end of my paper days when I refused to deliver anymore and hid the plastic wrapped stacks in my fort, I would bring to you, Pearl, your paper—never knocking.

Pearl, your reply that August Friday afternoon was garbled as if speaking through a door. As I stood on the edge of your living room, balancing on the wood threshold above the lower enclosed porch next to the upper oak desk. I could tell your voice came from towards the bedroom.

Pearl, I thought maybe you were in the bathroom, which rather embarrassed me. So Pearl, I called out to you, that I would leave your unfolded *Valley Journal* on the inner oak desk. On Saturday, Pearl, we received a frantic phone call from Eleanor Moore, who owned your home, and her son Bruce would later live in your home with his bride and raise two girls.

You were supposed to make their wedding cake, but Pearl, nobody had heard from you as it was now their wedding day. Dad and Mom ran next door and quickly found you, Pearl, on the bedroom floor, having fallen, hitting your head severely. Blood nearly dried had pooled around your soiled clothes. We boys were told to stay in our yard and not come inside your home, Pearl.

Pearl, I stood in the hedge gap and watched the ambulance pulled up onto your gravel drive and then roll you on a gurney into the wagon that took you away to a hospital far south. Monday morning, Mom woke me to talk with Dad while he shaved. Pearl, he told me you were dead. That you never woke up again from the fall.

Pearl, I was ten then, forty-six years ago, when you passed at sixty-five. As I'm near your age as I knew you, Pearl, I find that particular Friday afternoon in August haunts me. Pearl, instead of embarrassment, if I had found you splayed on the bloody floor and run for help you might have lived a few more years of my youth or even enjoyed a long-lasting life.

Ironically, Pearl, great-grandma Norris passed that December at 91. In the aftermath, my parents culled some rows of your treasured books. Pearl, over time, Damnit adopted us, coming into our home to eat and drool in our laps when happy.

Pearl, we had to have your sweet blind toy bulldog Gordo put down.

Pearl, we lost access to our forts after we gathered any prized possessions and rarely ever moved through your home, where once, Pearl, our freedom was never questioned.

Pearl, we watched the Moore girls grow up in your old home.

Pearl, all your possessions are gone, although, I still possess the white pottery owl with black lines, from Acoma slate of Sky City which we bought that same June summer in Kayenta as a gift for you, Pearl.

Pearl, we savored and lamented the last bottles of that zingy catsup the color of sun-dried tomatoes.

McGovern lost that fall, Pearl. Over the years that well-placed bumper sticker faded in the seasons of life.

As I realize nowadays how close my own death stalks,
when we finally meet, Pearl,
I hope you can forgive my childishness,
my foolishness,
my inability to do more than to hold
your pottery owl in hand,
my Pearl.

## Caught in the Nick of Naked Time

A transitory troika
caught in the nick of naked time
black dressed, voices spouting
visceral lockjaw drug-speak
beech wood block 12-pack bottles
or pure Nazi rocky mountain spring water
garage read/record full color photos
aren't/weren't we a piss full of death.

In this troika
Ricky Williams, too weird for Flipper
such a Crime to be booted for Quaaludes
long scraggy hair, gagged on a plastic spoon in Agnew
State Hospital, recorded with the Sleepers, Toiling Midgets, and with
Tom Barry, too quiet for some but giggled much on shrooms, painter,
inventor of City of Fear card game, pen and inker of Manson and
myself, so wasted holding my whale harpoon inherited from Clara Baber,
looking away for all the wrong reasons.

A tombstone, a crypt plaque and my naked dizzy head
I'm the only one to outlive the parents, "Loving Son." O
I'm no loving son, but a lover of life, and so much closer each day
to being in the ground where my ashes belong. The owls are not
what they seem, our mantra giggle and the log lady, hell, cut another
line. Using the hatchet blade, a self-referential poetic joke. Ricky
took the camera, shot a pic of TB and me pissing.

**Looking Away for all the Wrong Reasons spring 1989**

(back to front) author, Ricky Williams, Tom Barry

## Frogs Are Easy to Find

The frogs of the old horse
pasture are easy to find.

Once you got there— walking
down the creek bed of cattails and rushes.

Once you walked down the old
railroad tracks that cut through

the neighborhood that a train hadn't
used last week or in decades.

Once you walked past the donkey pasture
that abutted the railroad track, which

continues onward by the VA hospital and the
old dilapidated barn in the distance falling apart.

Once you got past Matadero
Creek's bridge and had turned down

Barron Avenue towards the redwood
lined school with the wide open yard.

Once you passed the pine tree and turned into
the driveway of your home, by passing

the front door, for the side door by the kitchen
and below the kitchen window towards the

back gate on the concrete slab. Once
where you saw the frog's body decomposed

over days. First, losing its rubbery skin,
then its muscles and guts. Finally, down

to its delicate bones before finding its way
into the paper lined trash can.

The older boy said, "Frogs are easy to find."
And he threw the beast as hard as he could

into the creek. "But I want snakes!"
And when he left, you recovered the dead.

# What People Wanted Me to Do

Dad wanted me to be a business major.
I got my degree in creative writing—
I knew the thought-provoking classes, the easy A
and the people, this community my folk.

Mr. S— wanted me to sell condos for his realtor business
—he said, I was a natural. I met the team once, a guy with
patchy ruffles around bald pate, a young woman in a black
coat over a green blouse with slacks—non-descript.

Kevin wanted me to climb the Gunn High flagpole. Seniors, we
were. Sheer metal pole had holes to the top. He had given me four pegs
—once up, set up a pulley and drop the climbing rope, then haul the
Bob's Big Boy statue they had stolen and impale it on the pole top.

Tom Barry wanted me to slip into the Palo Alto police
station from the Ramona Street side with a package.
I was to avoid the cameras, and leave it inside the building
                              —then run like hell.

I didn't. I wouldn't. I couldn't do
any of that crazy shit. Hey—a business
degree is crazy. I do what I do.
        —That's crazy enough.

# Rocks

Take rock out of pocket, *Schlag*
one more time, *be true today.*


toss stonegrain square to square, hop, bend,
pickup school's reroof gravel, desk kept.


Shadow on blacktop shifts
mo(u)rn; "Apollo chariot overhead."


Stone weight, Sisyphus drags
out Robb Jackson's stoners.


Mailbox, blew it up. New box
Post. For luck, a quarter & pebbles.


Carry heartstone culled. Tara
pluck white rocks, black bones.


Next to the stick, rocks.
Colorado River tumbled smooth,


from the muddy floor, hope—
graceful man with big rock.

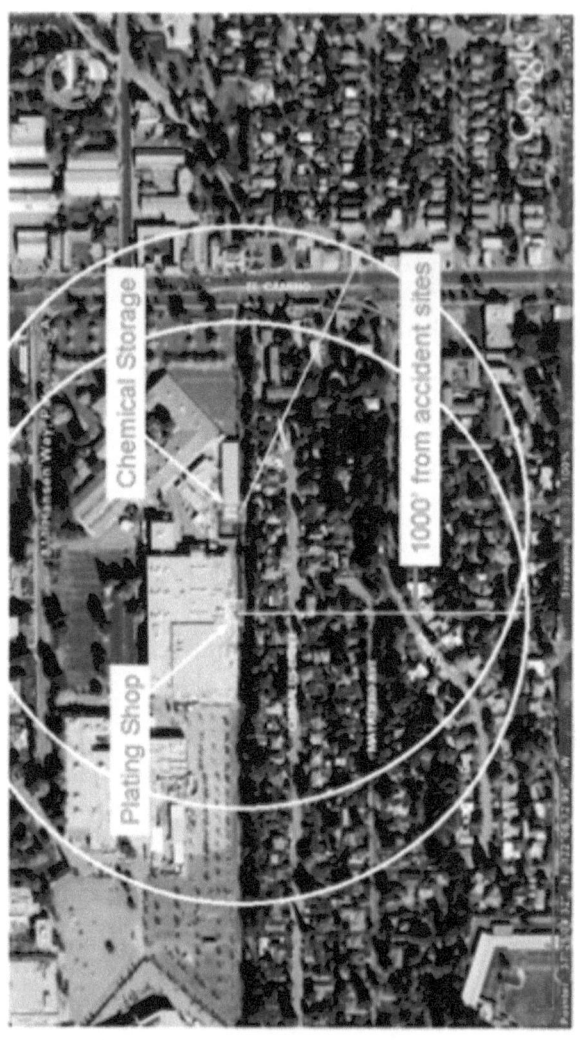

Art Liberman 2/19/07 Area Graph
http://www.bpaonline.org/artliberman/artliberman.html

# Brain Tumors of Barron Park

It's forty-four frickin degrees outdoors.
Wind blows, scraping one scraper
with another, thinking about the
three brain tumors of Barron Park.

Three of my generation.
Scott Fessenden as in *Fez*.
We and Matt drove the Southwest
in '81 at nineteen—the Grunt Trip.

Winter break from UC Davis
Twenty-one and ready to go
out for the night. Seizure
in a car. Luckily Fez wasn't driving.

The invasive biopsy-surgery.
Pinpoint radiation treatment.
Never went back to college.
Worked at a recycling plant.

Summers as Forest Service fire crew.
John Muir beard and dead at forty.
Tracy Olson, Pop's girl
       Gone at fifty.

Now Leslie Wickham announced
she too has a brain tumor. As kids,

barefoot, we traipsed Matedero
Creek—you couldn't keep us out.

Living next to Stanford Industrial Park
before buildings built. Horse pasture meander
for pollywogs along another creek now buried
from the heavy metal and the leaching.

Some dads worked for Hewlett Packard,
Fairchild, Watkins Johnson & Varian.
Syntex was further up the watershed,
nestled beneath Round Top.

Acrimonious, my cold fingers scrape
cracked Spackle and acoustic ceiling foam,
scraping up the unpleasant news
of the brain tumors of Barron Park.

# Steve Wilhite

What was your gift
to draw young boys
into your bed

getting them started
on patch trading
providing them beer

free movies
a place to hang out
an ear to listen.

With so many near in camp
only the pines creaked.
We were quite alone

in the director's cabin
dressed and on your bed.
You comfort me tight

three years after Bump's hand
woke and scared me in a Comanche tent,
grabbing my fourteen-year-old cock.

I expected your move
I was wanting your move.
Nothing happened—refused again.

# Fifth of November

Too many years ago today I was to end my life
with a can of Aqua Net sprayed into a plastic bag.
Huff it all.
Smother the lungs and choke to death.
Gasping for life.

I bought that can and stashed that bag in the garage.

It stayed there for a while.

On the sixth, I became a forger
accompanied with shaking lies.

And a friend saved me,
helped calm me to fit my skin.
It took a long time to find the perfect

look. The can and bag went to the dump.
I may be still shopping for them
today.

# Your Barron Park

Did you walk down Paul Avenue
or La Para, El Centro, Josina, or Ilima?
Did you tarry on Julie Court?
Did you go down Kendal, Tippawingo,
Magnolia or Military Way? Did you take
the private road between Chimalus and
Matedero after hanging out at the Flamingo
Motor Lodge playground before riding the elevator?

Did you want to grab some muscle, open up
your gears, speed down Los Robles, or
Laguna, bike across the old tracks on your
way up to the heights of Matedero Hill,
gliding down through time and space
—wind whipping your face?

Did you ride your bike to Driftwood Market, read
comic books in the wire rack by the office door,
where Pete and the butcher knew you by name?
Did you ever have root beer or 7 Up
slurpees that have never been equaled, where
candy came and went for a penny each?

Did you climb valley oaks' wide boughs
high off the ground, hard as the adobe earth
to see alabaster light of the stars? That rough bark of
our times—protests and war—lighted peace symbol

suspended in redwood trees seen from all of Barron Park.
Did you make your way down Matedero Creek from
Laguna to Matedero, looking into everyone's backyards?
Did you climb through the culvert bars next to Donny K's
to crawl Barron Creek tunnel to El Camino's far side?

Did you play off the ground tag or
kick the can into the summer night?
Did you doorbell ditch, or push a
car down La Para onto somebody's lawn?
Did you climb the pyramid of BP's lunch
tables that somebody stacked overnight?
Did you get up predawn to climb the structures
at Jonna Briones Park, or bike down to
Taco Bell to climb the back ladder to the roof?
Did you watch your friend's mother die?

Who stole our flag on the 4th of July?
Did they burn it or wipe their ass,
or cut up sections to bury their dog?
Here comes Norman B— barreling
down Barron in his wagon hosed down by Joan.
Did you sleep one summer night on cots
in Oly's backyard with T the night of
Thea's slumber party next door?
Laughing girls much older than we
skinny dipping that we watched
between the fence slats—T looked
once then said to get away from there.

They could be a mean crew—shot Meme's
dog dead on its own front porch from a
bedroom window with a pellet gun.

Did you go to the Axe House that became
Rudolfo's where you drank a bottle of Zin
with your underage future wife?
Did you go to the Iron Works where the
wait staff all wore denim even the skirts,
before it became Compadre's where you
did shots before your wedding ceremony?
Did you score some tacos at Taco Tío? Mr.
A—s's coin shop six lanes across the way.

Did you park your car on Chimalus, Timlott,
Shauna, San Jude, Paradise or Laguna Court
for a chance at some young nookie
or did you get pulled out of the car
by the cops when on the backseat naked?
Separated and questioned,
to be let go with a warning
that she's underage.

Do you remember all the massage parlors,
Linda's by the meat market and Togo's
across from Shakey's Pizza time theatre,
one by the laundromat off of Kendall
or the Kopenhagen Burlesque Theatre with
completely nude dancers where fathers went

at the other end of the dry cleaner's strip mall
where your dad's shirts and slacks were pressed?

Did you cross El Camino to J & D's Market
beneath Ali Baba's massage parlor with a
staircase that no one used in the light of day?
Did you buy your first six-pack of Lowenbrau Light,
then asked by the clerk, "You have ID? Ha ha ha!"?
Did you ride your bicycle home with your brown
bag balanced on the bars when you were just fourteen?

Did you know of the wife swapping parties?
The parties of fisticuffs. Those that didn't party.
The quiet of the neighborhood endured.
Rosemary, I think of you and Big Jim
in that chaos—an eye in the maelstrom—
there was always room for anyone between
the creeks in that ranchero slaughter house—
Matedero and that cattle fortune Edward Barron.
The epicenter of the Barron Park Bobcats realm.

# Not Weird Enough

Not weird enough, the asshole lived.
My pipe bomb friends, my hooker lovers
how, I ask, does such a Hep C infected
still survive? Either I didn't understand
the problem, or I sold out in such way that I no
longer was lonely enough to imbibe unrestrained
to destroy what I knew, see, I saw destruction,
grew—more like stunted—the destructive Col.

And then there is the ring. The ring. That is how
the asshole survives, marriage, kids, inquiry,
surprise, wonderment, excitement, unconditional
love, there was, is, betterment that the weird
could not connote the pain to carry on.

Still, a parasite, truly living off other's hopes.
Yes, to it all, keep me alive another day. No,
I'm not falling apart, that's banter beyond
anything, it's just the moment that feeds
but nourish? O no longer does that happen
shit(e) me, I cannot, will not expect to do
my share except dine and dash the mushroom
burgers.

# If You Took Anything from Berkeley

If you took anything from Berkeley,
it wouldn't be a large brown paper bag of pot
found in a woman's apartment with a wall mural

depicting a close nit birch tree
forest peppered *avec* demons,
but "Ecstasy." Hans Hoffman's

60" x 68" blue perfect, 1947, oil
on canvas *skrik*, orgasmic yellow
throb push pull in a green arm embrace.

If you took anything from Berkeley,
it wouldn't be the U.S. Navy's flight
demonstration squadron Ángeles Azules

llamados, mere circus sky-barkers
for the multinational military industry
complex, but University Avenue ripped

up by Governor Reagan, leaving nowhere
to demonstrate the lack of rights, plus
SFSU's gun-turret-pomo-University Center,

*sans* former large grass stretches, now slight
rises for sniper fire and easy body sequestering.
If you took anything from Berkeley,

it would be drinking Schlitz Bulls talls
hopping the fence at the 3rd Eastern Front
punk show on the shoreline with Suicidal

Tendencies and Black Flag's Greg Ginn's
guitar ripping air. If you took anything
from Berkeley, read Floyd Salas' broadside

"Pussy, Pussy, Everywhere," a revolving
bedroom with multiple tasty women dancing
in a green garden with yellow flowers

in springtime or late December,
and the tombs of dogs and cats loved.
If you took *anything* from Berkeley,
it would be the comment overheard at Cody's
on Telegraph: "She's more excited
about the new carpet than her fiancé."

# Graham Thomas *Lonicera periclymenum*

We called it honeysuckle.

Vines thatched the kindergarten

fence. For hours—it seemed—

plucking the white fluted flowers

sucking out the sweet nectar

as if we were bees

# The Transitory Troika

Moi is all that is left
of the transitory troika
that met in a Lancashire Tavern
brawl over a woman.

Not a very good-looking woman,
but young at the time
while they were older and oddly enough,
I was not involved in the initial debacle
of that pet of a child-woman. No, it was TB
or Tom Barry, mostly known around town as Tommy.
Later we were known as Tom & Tom. The woman

had been with this long black-haired guy
in a motorcycle jacket that matched his hair.
As I sat on the bar stool drinking my pint
of New Castle Brown, TB said, "Ricky, Ricky
of the Sleepers." "Who?" I didn't know the Sleepers
until Mr. Ricky Williams was laid to rest from choking
from that plastic spoon stuck in his gullet at Agnew State Hospital.
Yes, it was said it was a "respiratory infection." Hard to get over a spooning,
especially if it's a heroin overdose.

# Lower Barron

One of the oldest sections of Barron Park as evident in a 1948 photograph. Road once led to the California Military Academy. Barron Avenue narrows before La Donna, first curve to the left and slaloms to the right, hugging the curve in the street where smaller houses with deep narrow lots, some built for summer homes, for city residences—get out of the fog belt and chill where Mark Twain said, "the coldest winter day he spent was in July in San Francisco"—down the peninsula in a cottage on lower Barron.

At the corner of El Camino de Real next to a car repair shop was a turquoise half round building, once a dry cleaner, a kite store, an independent package sending location—hot-diggity-dog. Façade changing over the years, chipped but still there today. Dad drove us all up towards home fast, passing Jerrold and a young black man, who stood on the blacktop edge in front of the Felice's home, Jerry's home—we missed them, inches to spare—the black man spun around as I turned to look, double fingers and rage—on lower Barron.

A late dinner on the opposite side in the Smith rental home. Bill, a year younger, had already gone to bed after playing "Suicide Is Painless" on the clarinet. Rea, his mom, was having a good time and spilled her wine. Her husband, not Bill's dad, dragged her into the bedroom. Screaming. He came out and said, "Sorry." Mom and Dad and I said goodnight. In the car, starting to back out, Rea came out—grabbing keys out of her leather purse while crossing the lawn.

He came again and dragged her back into the house on
lower Barron.

Later, in the late 80s, English X lived across from the old Felice home.
X had bought the Tavern downtown from his cocaine dealership. In that
house X was indicted for child molestation of his two-year-old daughter
but after a decade of ownership it was time to sell and sell for cash only,
X had said, when we tried to broker a deal—it was good that bar sale fell
through. X planned to skip bail to play soccer in South America.
Instead, he called the cops, told them his big plate of coke had been
poisoned by someone. If only the paper article had his picture too, on
lower Barron.

It was a pretty peaceful walk to the closest bus stop, to take the 22.
I would ride it to Stanford shopping center and transfer for Santa
Cruz Avenue where the psychiatrist told me to beat a couch—
then got on the floor and showed me how it was done. He only charged
$125 a session—well worth it since I'm still here. I also took the 22
to work at Crown Books, and everywhere else around the Bay Area
but I broke apart when they chopped down the trees behind the bus
stop bench and across the vacant lot behind the car repair shop on
lower Barron.

# I Know the Day I'll Die

I know the day I'll die.
Someone will say
that Darwin was right,
it's survival of the fittest.

All I really can say to you
is something said by Camus:
The only philosophical question
is suicide.

These thoughts squirm in my brain
so I drink and snort cocaine.
Now their voices have no one
to listen.

# Ruggles and Bukowski

1989 was a pivotal year in my life.
Out of a relationship, out of a job, left school
and out of San Francisco,
I went back to Barron Park
            October 1988.


The job came quickly and so did the strife at home
built on lies, drinking gin, snorting cocaine.
Still trying to maintain some semblance as a writer.
I put out the first issue of *Box of Words* in November
1988, having to get writing from those I know or knew
at the time, like on 7th avenue in SF after making all

the arrangements, I came to the door of the poet
Eugene Ruggles of *Life Guard in the Snow* fame—he
remembered me from *Close to Home* but he forgot about
our meeting—papers strewn across his studio apartment
floor—palm up gesture wave towards the papers—"Take what
you want." I began sifting through the leaves of poems as Gene

went to the fridge pulling out a 16oz can of Green Death,
Rainer Ale. He sat on the couch as I read poems, "She is with April,
1988," "It's Your Grave My Friend," "Sounds" and "The Courage to Love."
He sat with his liter of vodka and his tall green can of ale.
When Gene tilted that cheap vodka back—guzzling continuously
until a third or more was drained—I'd never seen anyone drink

so hard before or since—he finished tippling and grasped Green
Death and slugged that can down as well. Before I left Gene's
studio—the only time I was let in—he was on his second bottle
and third can and it was not far past the noon hour. He eventually
sobered up, supposedly. Moved to the Petaluma Hotel shortly afterwards,
became Sonoma County's Poet Laureate, dying before being evicted

in 2004. Maybe Ruggles had already moved when I left a few copies of
*Box of Words* on his step when no one answered that 7th Avenue bell.

It was early April or late March that I was staying with my brother
and his fiancé in Costa Mesa when I borrowed Denise's Toyota MR2.
That red minx of a car was a babe magnet and I picked up a hitchhiker
on the way to San Pedro and took her on in the front seat—then she asked
for $40. I was game and tossed her the cash; I had no one then. I didn't care.

On a quest to get Hank Bukowski wild writing for issue 2 of *Box of Words*,
I knew he lived in San Pedro, near enough to the docks, so I went to the
bars and asked if anyone knew Hank, Hank Bukowski, the writer—no
one did. None had heard of him in any of the bars I visited on Gaffey
Street. I gathered my beer change, because it was obviously a drinking
day. Already laid once and another time to come. I called Floyd Salas in
Berkeley and asked him for

Hank's address and he willingly gave it to me. I drove over and knocked
on his door—but nobody was home so I left a copy of the 1st issue with
a note, asking for a submission. Then back to the bar, more drinks and
began to play pool with some women. I had read early in the year, *Ham on
Rye* and had started Bukowski's novel, *Women*. They had been published

within the last decade and I ate them up with Hank Chinaski. I fell in with a heavy Mexican woman who like

jokes and my dapper clothes—it didn't hurt that I was buying her drinks and shots. We ended up on the waterfront's stony breakwater, where we engaged in sex on the rocks—afterwards, I thought to try once more—drove back to Charles Bukowski's home and parked on the street. A bit disheveled, I straightened up as any drunk can and came up the drive to his home. The copies and my notes were gone, car in the drive. I rapped the door with my knuckles. It took a few moments but he opened the door—

he was shorter than I, by a good five to six inches with a white towel wrapped around his waist and another white towel wrapped around his chest—a bit of a homemade robe of sorts—after his shower. I said my name and I enthusiastically mentioned wanting a submission of his work to publish in *Box of Words*. "I threw that shit away," he said. I was shocked by his brashness. "You want it?" "Yeah, I want it." "I'll get it," he said and walked away to my left—in his home—with the door still open I followed a few feet behind him

into his kitchen, hearing rustling sounds. At the far end of the kitchen, Bukowski was on his knees. His hands and arms deep in the white garbage can and then he stopped and looked at the ceiling. "I can't believe he's in my kitchen," he spoke, then yelled, "What the fuck are you doing in my kitchen!" He was on his feet coming towards me. "Get the fuck out of my house!" He threw the issues and note at me and I pointed my finger at him, "Fuck you, Bukowski! Fuck you!" The little man in white towels charged at me, but at too much distance to grab me as I quickly fled his house, turned again and the door was shut tight. Down to the street and Denise's red MR2 with *Box Of Words* in my hands and I thought about my failure—and thought that I just told Charles Bukowski to fuck off. I went back up the drive to his door and knocked again—his wife Linda opened the door. "Hank he's back! He's back!" I waited at the door. The threshold held me in check and he came once again to the door. "I'm sorry, Mr. Bukowski! I'm sorry!" He kept his eyes on me and quietly said, "Yeah, that's okay." And then the door closed with a click.

The deadbolt slid tight with a clunk. Slowly back to the car, I drove back to Costa Mesa after a booze and women-filled day, trying to get words from the creator of Hank Chinaski. I stopped working on my idea of painting Hank Chinaski in the back of the streetcar with his head bandaged from boils—smoking a cigarette with the stern eyes of hunting hawk searching for a kill.

# Wong Manor

The field was open
Split rail fence
Staking the claim
Between road and dirt
Sold off to Asians
For their dream home

Paid cheap labor to dig
Foundation trench by hand
Turned out a half-
Foot short of code
Had to lower top floor
By as much

Stucco and brick box building
Concrete yard surrounds
As it was built
We used to party
Huddled quietly
On wood subfloors

Inside Wong Manor
Drinking and snorting
Pissing in closets
Throughout the night
Reclaiming what was once
Open space of youth

# The Cockroach's Worth

The cockroach's worth
Annihilation of the filth
Age dims eyes slower than brew
Unsent letters, unfinished work
The megalopolis juxtaposition
A single bark strand earth touch
Even this pome reeks rank

O the weapons
                          Oil change in Sienna
Asheville beers
                          Flying double disk clouds
Over Cold Mountain
                          Collide ekonomikos
Bridges burned
                          Crime of existence

Not knowing more about M. C. Richards
        Higginbottom is a funny name
Laughter is joke away
Like the groundhog's dash
On the knoll within sight
Of Tom Wolfe's grave
Yes, it's not Thomas it's Tom
                          The bon mot here
Not another fist to shoulder
                          A punch to the deltoid

Only a ~~jarhead~~ could create such amusement
    Swinging dick

The society page women
    Failed literature

More interested in the tweets
    Than life love death & sex

Cadre of gal-pals
    The punting puce

The brothers, public service
    Public enemy, public

Hatred of the pig's head
    A penchant for pomes

Dastardly trade
    Sticks to sweeping

Mows deep thought
    Dream, no future

## Secrets and Lies: Father's Confessions

                                          In Barron Park
where the real Nurse Ratchet lived
people were lawless, broke vows—
stole partners, burgled and committed suicide.

Secrets my father confessed,
the lies he professed over the years
at the kitchen table, I could bury
in the ocean like Ahab or Osama.

To loosen these lips and sink to the bottom of the pond
willing to be beaten like Bob Crane with his own tripod
or if lucky, take the single shot in the back of the head
Floyd Williams style.                                 "Barron Park"

My father chimed. "People called it a 'golden ghetto.'" I
panned Matadero & Barron Creeks fruitlessly, trickle water,
huge rough bark oaks on the banks, dead leaf duff and poison
oak—a thoroughfare for kids through solitude and leaf carpet.

Secrets the father confessed under alcohol—beer (Coors),
wine (Cabernet), scotch (Cutty Sark/Glenlivet) and Drambuie.
There's sodomy, sexual abuse, domestic abuse and rapes
a cigarette always lit, gray smoke rising in single columns—

billows skyward, clustering into clouds about the ceiling
hypnotized by his voice as I stare at the kitchen witch

strung above the sink, turning round to stare back—later I drank
with him, piecing together the trifecta: the Corp / the abuse / the sex.

It starts out innocently, how someone had rolled a piano out for a late
night jam session party on El Cap Beach in Yosemite Valley. Living in a
Camp 4 (Lower Merced) tent for the summer, Fire Fall each night—burning coals streaming down the face of Glacier Point—then the band would
start up

The Camp Curry dance—a lifeguard at the pool at 14 during the war
had heard from a car radio at Mirror Lake that the Nazis had invaded
Poland—thinking, "What that means to me?" I think he tagged
that last bit on later. One lie down. So many more to sift through.

Some of his stories, they were stories at times, were funny too. Like his pool
sharking times up Humboldt coast way riding his Harley with long slicked
back hair—living game to game, town to town, 17 to 18 years old—a pack
of smokes rolled up his short white sleeve, undershirt—his aviators came
later on—past the

1st wife and my dead half brother, Kenneth—who it was just as well he died
at 6 months–SIDS–otherwise he would've been laid out in a body bag next
to Jerrold Jerry Vesey in Nam or swallowing exhaust in the car with Oscar
Krause or in the plane mountain crash with Bill Hastings—none of whom
ever heard a note of Quadrophenia—

watch Nixon wave goodbye, hear that the master of Middle Earth, J.R.R.
Tolkien had died. Never heard Band on the Run, the Paris Peace accord, the

taking of Wounded Knee, Roe Vs. Wade, OPEC crisis, dying in the Alaskan pipe, battle of the sexes, Agnew's resignation— mother fucker—if I seem cold, lacking empathy, where were you, when he interrogated me?

Over time it all came out—in the Korean War, after drinking from a stream, finding later upstream a dead body in the water and puking his guts out. His cannon cocker cock assurance mortar rounds a night patrol ambush laid out, him lying in wait for the last man's retreat to fall with his shot on top of him.

The nights out with his Japanese girlfriend whose father hated him because his wife and son were incinerated in the fire bombings of Tokyo.
The Korean brothel madame who came to see the general about canceling liberty stated, "You break my heart and piss me off."

Or the seven-year-old girl in some sand-pan dive bar that reached up and rubbed his penis until he was convinced to have sex with her—at seven!          Your oft-repeated joke, "When she says, she's only thirteen, say you're not superstitious."

Or when your aunt caught you in the middle of shagging her daughter at sixteen.          How many women could stand against you today to claim #metoo—There's the babysitter when living in Menlo Park—you said you tagged her. The two

Quist girls next door in Grand Junction—one of the three reasons you claimed for us to move back to California back in 1965.
How many women and girls—yes, I know how you liked them young—in Barron Park alone could scream #metoo to you!

## Kiss the Boot

Ya've got four or five lumps
of coal deep down that stocking
toe, ya'd better get limber to play
a round or two of Kiss the Boot.

Sock stroke the bully's face, sing
That jingle, rub raw their façade,
Singin' till that bully beats you
Off like swarms of gnats, ya give

'em Townshend's windmill
arm-swing gob-smack,
singin' that twinkle eye tune,
Kiss the Boot. Kiss the Boot.

When they stagger to the floor,
Circumnavigate 'em another cycle
Kiss the Boot. Kiss the Boot.
Once or thrice over the head,

It's time to be polite and sing,
Kiss the Boot. Blood splattered
Everywhere, slickens the floor
Playin' Kiss the Boot. Kiss the Boot.

# Halloween

> "That Halloween spirit came from the Civil War, soldiers marching at night with pinecones on bayonets aflame could become an unruly crowd."
>
> Col CL Murphy USMCR

*Part I*

They came with egg cartons in their hands
meeting at the elementary school across the way.
From the street they pelted the house front
while we watched black and white television.
The sound on the façade startled and scared us.
Pulling back the curtains as shattered egg slid down the glass pane.
Another hit again and again—whooping from the street.
Told to get out of the room and go to our bedrooms.
Mother comforted us as he called Major H, the assistant Cub Master.
Then he went outside into the night with malice in his heart.
The attack did not daunt just pissed him off as he steeled himself
around the car to bolt into the street—dispersing
the crowd of young men and nabbed one of the offenders.
His grip was of thirty-one strong and he clutched that boy tight
whose screams made him sound like a girl as he was dragged
indoors and shuffled into the kitchen—his red hair and tear-
stained eyes, relaying his phone number in a quavering voice.
He spilled his guts—the Den Leaders of the Cub Pack he led.
His father came down the avenue to collect his wayward
son—they all came the next day to clean off the sticky egg yolk,
clear whites and shells off the desecrated home of less than a year.
Hatred burned in their deceiving eyes as they had poured paint

thinner into the bucket of water before they had arrived to clean.
Scouring the dark brown painted wood and panes of glass, leaving
blotches of color scrubbed off before being repainted a decade later.

*Part II*
Barricading before it got dark—moving the garbage can
to the backyard, angling the cars to the backyard gate. Handy was
a sawed-off thick dowel that rested on the drier for years to come.
But we were let loose to trick or treat — that first time as a ghost.
We were on La Donna—Chas, Wick and I—already told don't
take any apples since razor blades could be shoved deep inside.
Wick had on a monster mask and we all carried pillow cases to
collect treats. Then they came tearing down the street in a dark car.
Swish of eggs grazed my sheet, but Wick took them to the head.
Poor shots missed the white ghost to hit the one darkly clad kid.
The couple in the house were sweet to let us in as Wick bawled.
We were cleaned up, warmed up, and calmed down. Wick's
look at my costume forced me to remove the sheet and deposit
it into my pillow case. We edged our way home—taking Paul
to El Centro—never wore *Peanuts* white again on Halloween.

*Part III*
Bag full and left Jim's on Paul, feeling adventurous.
Went to La Donna to check out the action— a group
of marauders at the corner of Barron. They looked big,
mean and many that I dived into a patch of ground junipers
and waited for them to pass by. They didn't leave the corner

and I began to recognize some of the voices—so I fought my way out of those juniper boughs. They had homemade cannons, black electrical tape together three tin soda cans with a church key triangle vent at the end. Pouring lighter fluid culled from the folks and stuffing a tennis ball deep inside before shaking the contents up and down. When a car came down the road, they would Zippo light the vent—projecting their ball at moving car. My brothers and their friends were jubilant with their success.

*Part IV*
In the early 70s, Barron Park school became the place to be for Halloween action. By then, All American, Lucky's and Driftwood Market forbade egg sales to kids a week in advance of Halloween, though shaving cream and any fruit from the old orchard trees around were prime weapons to carry. We got home early enough for the real war that was across the street from home at Barron Park school. A crowd of seventy-plus people were gathered across the way when the Santa Clara County sheriffs arrived to disperse the hooligans—they went in every direction. Roger Vesey ran across the school yard, heading straight home, chased by a fuzz cruiser with its spotlight on Roger zigzagging all the way to the cyclone fence—he scrambled over and disappeared— into Matedero Creek behind his home. Others took off and were left to leave with a lineup of pigs in full riot gear, shields, batons and face masks as they marched the crowd towards El Camino. We stood near the end of our driveway, my brothers and others, when a sheriff asked who they were and with his parade ground voice, he told them they belonged here.

*Part V*

During the draught, a late-night arsonist burned part of Barron Park Elementary that changed the landscape when they fenced the property and yard as the school closed for repairs. That didn't stop any young males from coming to BP for — All Hallows Eve. They lined the small sidewalk further up and across the street—in front of Mr. A's house. Mr. A, an assistant coach of the high school baseball team and many there knew him. He sat on a brick post of the short picket fence to keep the peace with the testosterone-laden throng that threw eggs at a slow creeping station wagon. The screech of brakes echoed off the school walls. Ms. B got out and confronted the crowd of mostly young men. Seeing Mr. A sitting there among the group, she sauntered to him and slapped his face. Mr. A grabbed Ms. B's arm and said, "Lady, get back in your car." She coasted around the corner towards home. It wasn't more than twenty minutes before the Palo Alto Police showed up and chased the kids down Carlitos Court. Many ran to Wick's backyard fence. When twenty or so hit the redwood fence to climb over, the posts snapped and three lengths came down to the deck. Every kid scrambled to get inside Wick's house— the cops followed the crowd and went inside—handcuffing as they went every high school kid that they could roust from the rooms and closets.

*Epilogue*

To this day, I clean up my yard and park the cars as close in before trick or treaters can come out to wind through the streets, knowing full well where I put that wooden dowel.

## Brother Pneumonia

Kenneth, Ken, Kenny—can I call you Kenny?
Half-brother who lived and died the
Chinese Tiger cycle before I was born.
Kenny, you most likely died of SIDS, but you're
known among us as Brother Pneumonia.

On a chilly December night in 1980, Kenny,
our dad chased my mom out of the house.
Him three sheets to the wind confessed
that you had lived, Kenny, as I eavesdropped
and Chas listened, dad supine elucidated in bed.

In your crib sixty-nine years ago you died, Kenny.
My folks always celebrated September 16th.
We thought it was their wedding anniversary,
but who knows now when that moment took place?
Their mood seemed bitter-sweet, Brother Pneumonia.

Kenny could have lived to die on Hamburger Hill,
or been a Hashbury drug runner for a roadie of a scrappy
nowhere band or shacked up with Squeaky and ended
gutted by Tex at Spahn Ranch. Kenny, your multiverse
futures were fueled by poverty, my Brother Pneumonia.

Late spring birth, you lived across the summer of '50, Kenny. From
a cold to pneumonia. You broke your parents apart with your sudden death.
After the divorce, at a complete loss, dad ended up joining the Marines.

Kenny, I cannot fault you for any of these actions of sorrow.
They were two twenty-year olds knowing nothing about babies.

If you had lived, you would have changed everything, Kenny—
Dad's draft notice came later on. He would have left you in poverty.
My brothers and I would never exist—except for your sacrifice.
As painful to say and as cold as it may sound, Kenny,
my dear Brother Pneumonia, I'm glad you died so I may live.

# Too Much a California Boy

We wore cutoffs—made from
patched knee pants in summer
—went barefoot everywhere,
around the corner, the school yard,
even in the creek—bees love the
clover, but didn't like bare feet.

There were three of us
wearing cutoffs and t-shirts
Jeff B— also wore a bandana wrapped
around his head to keep his long hair
in place as he ran and kicked the soccer
ball—*fútbol en todo el mundo*—Chev and I
were on the back field of BP too—
a place for all kinds of pickup games.

The three of us kicked the ball around
together— it didn't matter at the time
that Jeff was fifteen, I was eleven
and Chev was nine. Winded, we
stopped to hang out at the fire pit
benches. Jeff whipped out a joint,
sparked that puppy up. I took it
and toked it, passed it on
to Chev, he followed suit.

# Rebuke

    I have bitter, empty and forlorn words
    for you. They shape and dissipate quietly
in the ever-present sadness grinding as gallstones
against each other, too large to pass, too sharp to
    forget as they collide, shatter and embed
        shards into the lining.

Your news was sobering, but I lost sobriety
in response to toast a fallen Fedora-bearing
hipster of the punk milieu, as we had so
often imbibed together, ran streets, bused,
booked and snorted that we called each other
brother—yet you are no father to me.

        It bothered your son,
Tom, knowing you were a Gestapo member
of Palo Alto High's draft board during
Vietnam, and that you made him as boy of 5
carry a Goldwater sign for propaganda.
        He would not like my rebuke and maybe it

    is self-indulgent, rather a self-rebuke. Nonetheless
    he's laid out in the ground next to your first wife.
Barry, your name-sake son junior, there will never be
a III in the lineage line. Tom told me about recording the
vehement arguments over the Vietnam War you and his sister
    had nightly over the dinner table. Rewind the reel to

reel and listen to voices of angst in the darkness, lights
out. He would take the picture of Ron and Nancy Reagan,
personally autographed to you, off the wall for us to cut
countless big fat coke lines to snort off their image. Then, after a
few beers, "I'll Meet You in Poland Baby" thumping the walls, discussions of
his house robbed, the family photos found soiled in Adobe Creek.

We hung out as Tom and Tommy, clung together.
People whispered 'lovers' the question had to be
asked. My tear spoken query, "Are we to be lovers?" met a
stiff shake of the head, a mute denial the question ever asked.
Your son was a rock of strength and danger for me in that
labyrinth he never escaped. Unlike Icarus, though many times high,

he never flew the coop, nor encouraged to grow
only enabled
to drink
to drink
to drink
to die.

# Terry Martin

I remember Terry Martin, Terry Martin.
His father was a longshoreman, had tattoos.
He lived just up the street, on Barron Avenue.

We were never really good friends,
Probably the better of friends.
Like when we were in second grade

I remember being in his home
With the big huge tree in the front
And the big huge tree in the back

The short small step into the house
And out of the house out in the back.

And then we had the fight,
The fight where I used wrestling moves
When I was in fifth grade—sixth grade—
And I kind of choked him
And I won.

Terry's
Crowning achievement probably
In education in any sort of way
was the pitch
The pitching he did
In our game versus the faculty

in elementary school
And he pitched
                a great game

And Rusty Berthiaume,
Our manager,
When I asked him
"Can I pitch?"
"No, I think Terry's doing really good."
And I have to agree
Terry did really good.

And the years went by, we really drifted apart
And there was a seething hatred
When we'd see each other

Terry with his white t-shirt
And his plaid long-sleeved shirts untucked
Dangling about his body
And the hatred in his eyes,
The nonchalance.


I don't think he ever graduated from high school
But I remember on his birthday
Which was always April twenty-second
Five days after mine
I remember seeing him
And this really said a lot about us

Since I was in the car with my mother driving,
Getting off Barron Avenue onto El Camino de Real
And I saw him—with his woman.
And I saw him walk away from his woman
                                              And his child

Who stood there
Who stood there
Looking at mother and father
Going in opposite directions
Caught in the middle,
Stood there
Not sure where to go
What to do,
And the child stood there
And this reminded me
Of Terry and his family
His brother Alan.
Well I have an older brother Alan as well.

Terry's brother Alan
Had polio.
Older
But with polio,
He limped up and down the road

And he was a
            thief.
In fact, the county sheriffs came

And arrested him
And others
Who were breaking into the house across the street from them
From Terry's
And arrested them and put them in jail.

It was his sister,
Terry's sister
And Alan's sister,
I don't remember her name
Linda, I think
But she had red hair like her mother
And she had actually called the sheriff.
Since we didn't have police where we lived
We had to get the county sheriff.
We were in an unincorporated area
In Palo Alto
Barron Park

And they came
And they arrested them,
Billy Deudney
And Alan Martin
And took them off to jail
And that was how the family was
A longshoreman for a father.
Working class
Trying to keep it together.

And Alan Martin was one big character.
When he was on LSD once
He drove his motorcycle
through Woodside High hallways,

Woodside
Driving that motorcycle.
He was a character
I don't know whatever happened to him
As he limped along
Down the street
From polio.

And then there was Terry
                        later
When I was in Floyd Salas' class
And we were eating pizza
At the Round Table pizza
On University Avenue in Palo Alto,
The one that Tom Barry used to work at
                        downstairs
Where he would have flour all over his pants.
You could pat TB's pants and flour dust would rise
Just like the pizza crust.

And then
As we were sitting there
Eating our pizza
After class

After our Monday night class
And having a beer
And I pointed to Terry
As he was coming in
To Floyd
And I said, "That guy hates me.
You back me up if something happens?"
Floyd being the boxer he is and was
Said, "Yeah, sure."
And he could see it
As he said to me later,
He could see the hatred in Terry's eyes
As Terry looked at me
And stared at me
And saw me
Right there

Right there in public,
Saw me
And the hatred burned in his eyes
That hatred going all the way back to that fight
That hatred going back to
Possibly
The advantages that I had
Financially and stability
And my family
But he didn't know what was going on with me
As much as I knew of what was going on with him.

And then, ironically
As Tom Barry and I
Digressed even further into our
Cocaine and crack habits
We ended up hooking up with Terry
And going back to Terry's old home.
His parents, the longshoreman
And his redheaded wife,
I don't know where they were then
Somewhere else obviously.
I didn't know where his woman was
Where his child was
I having none of those at the time

And so we ended up at his house
Smoking crack together
Talking and
Partying.
Maybe we had crank
I can't remember
But we were doing some type of white powered imbibing

And he talked
And he told us
Tom and me,
A wonderful scary tale
About him and his buddy
When they had stolen a car
And they were driving on Bay Shore Freeway

Down by San Jose
Heading north
And they were on PCP
And they started having delusions,
Delusions so bad
That they had to park the car
On the freeway.
They pulled off on the left-hand side
Of the fast lane
In the middle meridian of 101
And they were there
Having these delusions
On PCP
And they—Terry—
    Ran across the freeway
Skipping through
The buzzing traffic as it came at him
Barely making it
And as he got up
Over the overpass
Was actually walking over the overpass
Seeing the stolen car parked on the meridian
Down in front of him
Crossing highway 101
Trans the actual freeway
The vein of Silicon Valley

He watched his friend
Stumble through the lanes

And get hit by a car
Bounced
Careened
Caromed
Off cars
As if he were a pinball
Bouncing
Until he was down
And run over

That was the last time
I saw Terry Martin.
That tale
And we hung out
And partied at his house
And had a good time
Together
Like we did playing in his backyard
As kids
Running around
Playing games like tag
Or other things

But we had this magnificent tale
That Tom Barry would bring up
Again and again
About Terry and his friend
On PCP.
"That was a good tale," I said.

"Exactly. Exactly."

Where are you, Terry?

I have no idea.

Peace brother.

*Pylons*, 2010

# Lichgate *Diwan*

# The Last Days of Cherry

Isolated from the world,
we can't let her into general population
      —meaning the kittens —
Steph & Cass will attack her.

Cherry spends long days out back.
Meanders the bricks in umber—
"Stick to the shade like in Spain."
                      We the people

of cats, eagle claws. I know
they're talons, but Cherry's
are claws. Last of the older
girls, the other three died

months ago. Cherry's getting
there herself. Poor beast!
A tumor in her nasal passages,
bulging from forehead, keeps

left eye nearly open all the time;
a cyst bleeds in the upper
corner of her right eye. She bites
my pen as it tries to glean truth

of this wonderful girl. I want to
explain—to you, Cherry.

I think the bug guy that sprays
The baseboards and the house

perimeter, stirred up
by the gardener, could
have given you the crud
that makes blood splatter

out of your nose—I've
tried keeping the D'Hanis
tiles clean of your blood
to no avail. It's only days

left of your life. Such a
beginning: plucked
from hell's drainage grate
by Robb Jackson. Given

a home. What was the name
of that Maine Coon cat
that scared the shit out of you?
You lick all of us. Though you,

Cherry of days better, you've
found a place of peace. So
few find it. Too many gals
die earlier than should be.

There's Sparkle the Twitch.

Deaf Rosy, under the fridge
with her head. Blue—oh, dear
Blue—did I give you Sparkle's? —

—he took a sip of Shiner Bock
—Ellie came in to tell me, she's
done with the dishes and gave
me the thrice over when I talk

about this poem I'm writing,
on the last days of Cherry.
Cherry loves her ears scratched.
Has a powerful ribcage. Though

she cannot jump, Cherry pulls
herself up with the strength
of her front paws and muscular
front. I'm not shaking—she's

biting my pen—licks my hand.
I lol and I say, "awe." I kiss her
furry gold. Oh Cherry, let's
tell Rod Carlos Rodriguez!

Though I love you, I must
have done something to sprout
that tumor that bloodies your
breathing – yes, it's hard writing

with tail flicking over the page—
be good to José Angel Araguz's
*Small Fires!* I haven't read it
and it's on top of the pile.

—Oh, so sorry Blue, did I give you
Sparkle's Alpha Interferon B?
No, that was one of my shots.
Was it for allergies? No, it was

Insulin for Sparkle's diabetes.
Oh Blue, did I give you Sparkle's
shot? I swear I gave it to your
sister, though you're both black.

Or Blue, did you drink tainted rainwater
from the exterminator spray, pooled
inside the bedroom tray-track of the sliding
glass door frame where I found you dazed?

What else could it be? I'm callous,
a beast, an uncaring bastard! The game
pops back on the TV, Rockets versus
Spurs, game five. I love you Cherry

Berry. I was broken with Blue's death
and burial. Uncertainty of how haunts me.
Rosy's middle-of-the-night yowl calls me
to prayer. Oh, rest Sparky, my dear,

you're still my phone background.
That was sad to watch you waste away
from nine lbs, down so small—fighter
you— to four. Once a freight train

through the cat door. When you
refused to come to eat and sat
in protest on the monopole birdhouse—
staring from inside it. Bowl in two hands

lifted for you to sustain yourself.
I would do that for all I love
starting with my daughters—
and the women all die too young—

Bobby Hsi, Tracy Olson, Gina Reynolds, Lala,
Robin Frost Fetterman, Judy Taylor, Heather
Anne Courtney, Bobbi Chovanec, Danait Kidane,
Carla Jasberg, Janice Patnaude, Carla Berkich,

Jennifer Lynn Wood-Vanderheiden, Lisa
Borrall Evans Brown, Merritt Wikert,
Gretchen Troy Overton Burford-Dernetz

Pearl Krause, Molly Olgin & Jane Murphy.
Cherry, these are your last days.
You're laid out over my desk—
Rich Haswell will visit in ten days.

Alas— Kawhi Leonard injured.
The timeout is over, Cherry.
I may be tried for Blue—by my
own hand. Go towards the light.

It is easier to navigate. In the name
of the Rod, the José & the Robb
let us say a prayer for the gals—
                              —Ah.

# That Asteroid

That asteroid burns through the atmosphere
                          blazes and scorches the air
plummets in the Gulf of Mexico near Yucatán
like no other cannon ball-slamming the silted
bottom throwing steam and clay into the sky
like no other hydrogen bomb—the tsunami
follows the shock wave, killing off anything
that's still alive. Seventy-six million years ago.

The lingering stench long dissipated,
only the bones and fossils left. We've
tapped with long drill bits that mulch layer
of black muck we call oil—roughneck refined
that motors us about—choking the world
to best an ancient rock that broke open
the watered earth. Indeed, all our acts
are another repercussion of that asteroid.

# Guernica Gernika

In Bilbao having enjoyed the Guggenheim
I've decided on the spur of the moment—(Live
Loud, Live Long) Jim Spurr—to take the bus
to Gernika—April 26 1937. My mother

Jane Green Murphy, Elizabeth Jane Murphy
June 5 1937—April 26 2000. I believe there
is a connection since my mother was in utero
when the bombing of Guernica took place.

Today is fifty-one days past [divisible
by seventeen thrice—my numbers] my
mother's 78th birthday and ninety days past
her death day – I must go and am going.

The dead tree, but no definitive spot
to gaze, just a pall of the past lurking
in the halcyon and rebuilt buildings.
The people here living could have been

those babies born prior to the disaster,
or previous – if they were seventy-
eight plus. Now three old couples
have encircled me at these tables

in the *Escuelas Público*, Sunday
afternoon gatherings maybe happening

for decades like the summer Sunday
dances in Valladolid. Who's alive still

by Sunday? Who breathes, who
is ambulatory? Who remembers the Monday
bombs fell and shattered our lives?
Who remembers that day here,

Gernikan! *Paillartac Faxiso*! Alive
though hands shake! *Paillartac Generalísimo*!
They sing together, break their fast, have
*café con leche* and a beer. That's why

Gehry is so pomo! Swims up river to sparkle
a city mired by repressed life and fox hunts
for the ETA. Time to find an *aseo* and the
*autobús*! Back to Bilbao to unfold the mind!

# The Last Woman on Earth

I want to enter you as if you
were the last woman on earth

humble, honored, and bound
to seek mutual pleasure

so that gem-time
of this rarefied gift

would never fade. A final
opportunity to give a life

time of *jouissance*
only to watch the blush

of your cheeks fade
as an accompaniment

with the sunset
and the end of life.

# Lichgate

Susan has always claimed the want
to be buried at sea
ashes strewn like her father Herman's
by the Neptune Society.
"Over the side!"
Fantail detritus.
Slowly shifts with current and weight
towards seabed floor
if not mistaken for
guppy food descent.

No memorial location, fearful
frightened of no point of reference.
I wasn't sure of that fate
though the burning of flesh
pyre always the preference.

Though to the self
conscious zilch,
no dread in dead,
only among the living.

Among the beaches
sand cliffs
steep angle to surf.
Pescadero.
Pomponio.

Here at the crash,
clamorous loops of
pounding white water spewing upwards
and across the flat of sand.
I'm alive for the flood tide.
Finding no rest in active float.
Rivulets of surf popping bubbles
ebb home; this place I know.

Boogie-boarding Malaquite
saltwater lips
seaweed hair
as Odysseus, Witka & Thomas Just.
Zephyr the fanfaron.
Bejeweled tungols arc the welkin
the grandest, oldest, lichgate of all.
Pass, I shall.

# Corpus Sunrise

Sun breaks,
through liquid horizon -

magenta-
orange ball of flame.

Simmers
a shimmering disk,

ripple bay glass reflection
rises until liftoff;

superimposes its own
image skyward.

## 7 13 15 (Campo Grande)

I saw you between the hedgerows
straddling his thighs, arms around his neck,

on a wooden bench. Your eyes didn't meet—
no—closed to the world with mouths locked,

his hand wandering the expanse of your back.
In this darkness of green tendrils and squawk

of the peacocks, you're not the only frighten ones
to couple before others' prying eyes, now

lost in the rush of his pulse against
your close heat. He loves you, so he's said

and whether there is any truth in his
profession doesn't seem to bother your lips.

# Savio's Rubric

Mario Savio was headed to class at the Hutchins school—
silver mane long flowing, bound halfway down the back. Tall
and quiet strides message gentle recognitional wave, a short
nod "hi" passing through Mount Sonoma's shadow, on the
riprap paths skirting boulders, wood benches, smoking
student angst between Nichols and Carson, delineating
affirmative action's end and an added $300 elitist tuition
hike for SSU, quietly listening, to the Cuban gibbering
the chorus call, "ivy league west," cue up the antistrophe
response, "lay my body on the line," the final Greek
theater act blooms forth, the machine titters, the heart
beats on.

Call to arms, all citizens must be free, whether in
California or Mississippi, hunting humans with
thunder & lightning firesticks in the father river's
heart of darkness must cease and desist now.
The gold & ivory squanders be halted instead of we
the people. Walk a mile in Rubén Salazar's shoes
before his brains are splattered by a teargas canister shot
into the Silver Dollar Café and his name houses books.
Marj Gruzen heard Dr. King's calling, trek form NYC
emanating Rosa Parks' bus ride into Alabama to sleep
on different hardwood floors each night, dreaming—
the fire hose blasts and shotgun-toting peckerwoods from Selma
taunting "go home Yankee Jew." Lunch countering,
bathroom debates for free-flowing fountains and to walk

unhindered, unscared, anywhere the heart desires to
explore in passion. Floyd Salas called BS on the FBI
student infiltration at San Francisco State as Kay Boyle
Shouted, "Hayakawa Eichmann!" Boyle fired & Salas beaten
by the tactical squad's truncheons to stop the machine from
killing Charlie, from being stamped second-class citizens,
rising from under the fist of Johnson & Nixon's corporate
military madness with vox.

At the center of the civil rights centrifuge, Savio's
cadence cracked the clarion liberty bell, the white
supremacy anthill kicked down, exposing liars and thieves
scampering upon each other, grasping nest eggs in the run.
A young man pissed off at the autocracy university,
supported by Students for Goldwater and W.E.B. Du Bois Club
besides other legions in the first truthful American *Civil* War.
Empire arm murdering thousands in Vietnam, Chile, anywhere
to keep equality at bay ended in a whimpering resignation of
President Dick. Resounding depression crossed the nation
amidst parties that breathed a liberated fresh plowshare air.
Madness appeared squashed, but pseudo Dicks rose
in business as usual like poison ivy trimmed, not
uprooted. As Eastern Europeans cut the chains, fascism
reigns where white trash and the elite bind together again
as news of Central American death squads once called
fictional are revealed as truths, that American taxes bought
supplied & trained for business to keep extracting,
exploiting a dollar, squeezing life from peasants,
cardinals and hope. Cogs continue to grind human

meat, spitting dignity out between rust-stained teeth with techno-babble information fanaticism to devise a control chip. Go people! Go! Raise your voice! Spill your guts! Sing Savio's Rubric, "The machine will be prevented from working at all."

# Perfume Breeze

Can one inhale a thousand years—
Emirate of Granada, the Córdoba
Caliphate—Andalusian perfume.
Poor Selena, who knew not
women's freedom in the Taifa.
Wallada bint al-Mustakfi, blue eyed
and fair, hijab in public never worn.
Transparent tunics and stitched
robes words of grace and style.
Lover in the gardens of al-Zahra,
while under the arched columns
of the Mezquita or in the Generalife
—Alhambra, where water bubbles
can one still hear Mozarabic
spoken. The language for Muslims
Jews & Christians of al Andalus.

That al Andalus perfume breeze—
green Alhambra Reserva 1925 bottle
sweat, perched at terraced tables
of Taberna 22, on narrow Cuestade
San Gregorio's declivity, river
rock path skirting El Albaicín.
Crave the Darro, you grieve
the Guadalquivir of past nights.
I miss you, Wallada bint al-Mustakfi
like air by a fish at red tide,
like a Spirograph jet route map
without a legend to explain
Medina Azahara's destruction or
Al-Hakam II's library plundered.
While bamboozlers skim the crowds
pressed in for Romani square flamenco.

## The Last Time I was in Paris

The last time I was in Paris
at the back of the train

leaving Gare Saint Lazare
the sun setting over the Seine.

Boats on the river
cars and people in the road

the sun dropped
like a stone

into the bottom
of the world.

# ¡Ya basta!

Where did the EZLN fall?
Maybe respected life too much.
Could have gotten Las Casas to plead
against Sepúlveda again      bitter pill.

Cock Brothers and Monsanto shame
us to zip mouths with their chemical
cash. We're all digitally hooked. No
suckass end to the cops' color war.

When you start believing the pigs
are your friends that's worse than
Pacific Garbage patch! Corrupt FIFA,
         no different than Tom Brady's
saggy balls. My kids are growing up and

will inherit Gaia, deathbed edition.
Oh, love is not the problem, add a pint of respect.
Sancho and Isabella came together without
regret. Expulsion! Gaza Strip style. When the

Phoenicians came down the gangway, yelling,
¡Ya basta! Better buy! Give 'em *Strike*. "It's free."

# Hair (for Juan Manuel Pérez)

"I'm not giving in an inch to fear
    I promised myself this year"    David Crosby "Almost Cut My Hair"

The original punks – not the Pistols
punks that saw Iggy & Patty Smith
tours of '75 in San Francisco
who followed the Ramones—
those punks wore their hair long
Ricky Williams style

That's why I have long hair.
    I'm no damn hippie
I wanted to stand out
    Physically
after being called in my house
    Traitor
in 2004
because I was against the war
because I was against Bush & Cheney
because I questioned police when stopped
because I was so damn tired of the complete bullshit being shoved down
    my throat in the name of patriotism
because I refused to cross my heart during the pledge
because I would knee if subjected to Francis Scott Keys
because I refuse to accept the military industrial complex call to praise
veterans and grant discounts to military personnel and families because
they got mixed up in the cash for chaos post Twin Tower contracts

because my dad made me wear a buzz cut until I was eight in 1970—then only 3 inches long

because it freaked out my dad when I shaved my head during my punk heyday—that made him say—could you cut it any shorter?

because I want everyone to know that my long hair is a political statement of my unacceptance of the loss of democracy, the loss of civil rights for all citizens, the loss of protecting the environment rather than the business interests of the oil industry and those that want to strip the land of every particle worth keeping in its natural state

because even when I die or am murdered and they shave my head for their enjoyment—my hair will still grow.

## Dawn Moist

Dawn moist
petals unfold and spread
desire warmth, radiate
pulse with heat. Hot waves
blast across the humid morn.
Blinding light opens buds,
burns off frost to shake life into limbs
bent akimbo, tossed over or struck
straight into sky. Awaits
full slam of passionate sun
penetrate the darkest depths
and flood the tide.

## The Swagman's Bag

I once held the Swagman's bag
                         — lighter than air
with a finger and casual swing
                         hung that bag over me shoulder
the Swagman's treasure lightly pressin'
Atlas' smile on me mug
as I swagger that bag like Darby Crash
         jiggling a spike
                — gettin it all in
for the big dance up on the Sun


It was fleetin'
                — mere moments
Time's grains fallen'
             — no sweat
Swagman's Bag
              across these shoulders
If he ever shows
             'round here again
I'd be happy to buck
             — his load once more

# The Death of Jocelyn Jones

Documents spell out the demise of Jocy Jones, sexting
men, told a story—lead them to the palace of wisdom
with a wink. "Tell Jesus I said, 'Hello.'"
Dispelling the libel thumpers at the door.

Selling nugs and having to bum green, Jocelyn feral.
Repine, stripped shirt and unzipped skirt.
Russet vulva, bursting to be tied, choke to soak.

It was never going to end well, for Jocy, supine, waits
naked next to husband's snore creates an inability to chillax.
Ripped a bowl, adding haze to the dead appliance garage.
Oh! let my keel burst[1], she wrote onto a page of secrets.

Forlorn ablution shaved cooch and bespeckle ink.
Prurient Jocy pinches her nips to gush ready cleft.
Wanton titter, come hither repose eyes as drape thighs unfold.

Poison on wheels, wrestling through backyards,
towering fences, kicking the dogs, curvaceous,
taking it on the chin. Matching pistols with hubby's,
"I see a boy." She adjusts her skirt, "Glad you checked."

---

1   Ninety-third line in Arthur Rimbaud's "The Drunken Boat"

Wiggles *Exiles*, Jocy a brainiac flirt.
Hankers, educes, negotiates and procures.
"Darling, I'll never leave you."

O! How can LOVE exulting Reason quell! [2]
Wine glasses broken and a door smashed.
That son of a bitch wanting answers to her infidelities
though he couldn't bother to scramble eggs for their kid.

Cuckolded, he grasped the pearl handle, awaits her form.
In the early naked light, bullets sucker punch Jocelyn Jones.
Jocy spilt upon the wooden floor mixes life blood with guts.

---

2   First line in Mary Robinson's "Sonnet V" from *Sappho and Phaon*

# Who Can Forgive & Forget

Who can forget Checkers
        the gifted pooch
                of Watergate

Dickness of the summer
        of '74

Not the Republic of the unelected
        who provided the escape hatch
        from hard times
        prison bars
        in TV pardonese


Who can forget Crackers
        the mouthy
                Nazi pimp

and his hooker club
        Margo

Not Ripley's Believe It or Not!
        who provided the ontology
        of Vespasian's
        Urine tax
        in the Sunday comics

# Sonnet II

What task our utterance tilts
finger picks a rasp of metal into music
illuminates cloud edges with baked light
that juxtaposes night and day with cool dew
fills gaps of longing with heat passion lava
unburies the dead in the gray folds of mind
lures akimbo arms into hearten embrace
to leave us naked beneath holy stars
draws and quarters our bodies with charm and spin
sets sight sailing through corners of doom
drags danger under our skin airborne as breath
leaves us useless to quiver and mourn
pierces wind-driven giants to tap imagination
disintegrates the glaze of our kindly smile into earth

# Naked Panama Nights

> "In his sleep, naked Panama nights, the camera pulsing in blue silence and ozone smells, sometimes the cubicle open out on all sides into purple space" (William S. Burroughs *The Soft Machine*, 140).

Spectral goggles and orange antennae bluetoothing in carbolic soap
Glory holes in bathroom stalls — slo-mo close ups of green screen

Nights bordering on exploitation in Goya's el sueño de la razón—
Monstrosities of Johnny's gills and rectal mucus glowing in the bidet

Willy the Rat and Robert Kraft in Orchids of Asia blasting jism to KC
Cohen coughs up piss tapes of MAGA mothers of planet Strap-On

Hot nights of Panama Beach in the naked caffeine sale of ass for bed
Wiggle feet in the dog excrement water—before Vaseline spreads

Like priest prattle with pickpocket fingers boco abajo antennae sparkle
Blue spermy message—hot lick verbiage, "como perros" knees to nips

Sex hairs drenched, tossed salad before fracking the midnight oil
Up she rises, Billy Budd sings the limestone rag "Skinned Elbows."

Skinned Elbows—thought no one noticed that loving symmetry
Skinned Elbows— another night on the racking machine

# Lost Song of Pilar *(Canción perdida de Pilar)* *(for Javier Villarreal)*

In the *limón* house of Antonio Machado,
it seems years ago that he walked and it was

in Segovia, the simple layout upstairs
on the street of the abandoned and deserted

an open courtyard with stone path to the once
pension that held widower poet *próspero*

and his married lover, *Guiomar*.
They sip the mountains together.

With olive oil stove on floor boards
unfinished, between bed and desk

masks cracked paint faux baseboard.
Creaking with each step into the quaint

home Machado *llamado hogar por trece años*
yet, there did Pilar, *con sus tetas colgando al aire*,

stare into the dead bronze eyes of Juan de la Cruz
across the street as *tu poeta la tomó por detrás*.

Her robe pulled to the side that left her neck bare
she held the sill, "*Fóllame más fuerte; voy a terminar*

*a chorros.*" That dark diosa with velvet *vicio gemirá canto por la ciudad,* "*mi poeta, estalla dentro de mí.*"

# The American Axiology of Guns

The American axiology of guns
       bifurcates
              idiocy and inane

with ruby colored blood
       copper tasting
              pools and puddles

pavement and patios
       bathrooms and bars
              bedrooms and ballistics.

Justice doesn't wear a badge.
       She carries scales of balance
              fair and topless

tits of jealousy
       that liminal bang bang bang –
              cures nothing – disturbs

the ripped social fabric as it billows
       like Christo & Jeanne-Claude's
                    orange gates.

# I Am Eros

      I am Eros
      I am Death
      impregnating
      every spitting breath
      I smoke the joints
      on the moving street
      with a smile
      my shoes pound a beat
      I laugh at the gulls
      I tease the cat
      I pet the dog
      we all can chat

## Wedding Dress (for Don Luna)

After Helen was through with Aphrodite's
        Imperious curse, she gave Telemachus
a wedding dress, meant for Nausicaä.

He sailed wearing it on the voyage
to Ithaca—each night was his
wedding night—the men ravished
Telemachus from bunk to bunk
in the current.

On land with Odysseus—who bends
the bow—arrow shafts straight
from the quiver through the eye
hook of the axe handles.

Their immovable bedpost, Telemachus
two hands held to be whipped
by Penelope

        —who cross thatched
the warp & woof
of Telemachus'
        first dress—
    "When Nausicaä and I wed"

Telemachus wailed, "Arête can
tie me to the whipping post

for Blackdog Alcinous and his
seven sons—to lash me."

The suitors wolf-whistled.
Telemachus—unfettered and unashamed—
peered over his shoulder with hand

on hip, to yell, "What are you
boys waiting for? After all,
I'm Greek. You've seen the statues
of Apollo and Hercules, Zeus' son of lust
with his lion skin and club

for drag queens.
We can ride Argos around
the manure pile all the way
to the glory hole."

# Sacred Water (*Muwashshaha*)

Snow melt from España's Sierra Nevada
Pearl set in emeralds overlooks Vega
uphill from the Palacio del Generalife
*Con acequia y los albercones*
taps the Darro River eight kilometers away
Alhambra! – running water and cascades

> ReZpect our water
> Boycott Citibank
> Boycott Sunoco gas
> Boycott Stripes' tacos
> Dakota Access Denied!
> Defend Sacred Water

The Ancient Puebloans' water seeps
at the back wall of cliff dwellings
the lizards in the sipapu
chanting, "No fresh water on Alcatraz"
"Napa Valley blood soaked land"
"November 29th, 1864 Sand Creek lies"

> ReZpect our water
> Boycott Wells Fargo
> Boycott Sunoco gas
> Boycott Stripes' conveniences
> Dakota Access Denied!
> Defend Sacred Water

In the last decade alone
Sunoco 257 incidents of
pipeline releases, or liquefied
natural gas or gas from an LNG facility
Sunoco has the worst safety record
of 1,518 active pipeline operators

    ReZpect our water
    Boycott Energy Transfer Partners
    Boycott Sunoco gas
    Boycott anything from Stripes
    Dakota Access Denied!
    Defend Sacred Water

Sunoco owns Stripes – bought
all of them from Susser Holdings.
Both are owned by Energy Transfer Partners
who hired bulldozers that ripped up a burial site
who hired private security with water cannons
pepper spray and bloody-mouth guard dogs.
Fuck Facebook for its censorship!

    ReZpect our water
    Boycott Energy Transfer Partners
    Boycott Sunoco gas
    Boycott all Stripes
    Dakota Access Denied!
    Defend Sacred Water

Near the sacred Lake Oahe
Scared Stone Camp where all tribes meet
on LaDonna Brave Bull Allard's land to protest
while unarmed in freezing water
pepper sprayed and water cannoned
stand with Standing Rock ReZervation!

    ReZpect our water
    Boycott Energy Transfer Partners
    Boycott Sunoco & Stripes
    Boycott Citibank & Wells
    Dakota Access Denied!
    Defend Sacred Water!

# Richard Brautigan's Other Suicide

Why are we looking at the Golden Gate Bridge
from this perspective
as if we're on our way
down to the water

after having got
the guts to jump?
It *is* a nice foggy day
though. Foghorns play

an interesting melody in six,
no, seven tones; splat.

# 27 Julio 2015, Valladolid

I would rather be armless
    holding you
        in my sight

or breathless
    turning blue
        for my star tonight

car crash-painfully dazed
    restless on a lonely night
        a body blow I will take

if I can make you smile
    hear your laugh
        walk a few miles

Believe me when I do
    It's for life
        you're my wife

Susan, bright daylight of my world
    when we have time
        you're twenty-five

I'm better now
    ain't saying much
        you roll your eyes

I've been touched

        I'll say the most grandiose

                to hear your laugh    echo

                                      down

                                                      halls

## Scofflaw and Squander

scofflaw and squander
time again

across the wide bay
—rain bands

blue skies here now
—blinding orb

                                yesterday's videos
                                child's fort—chairs and sheets

                                playing horses
                                eating trail mix laced

                                with chocolate chips
                                there to film three girls

                                thirteen years ago—
                                humming as if bored

cat scratches door
wakes up alone

creaking ceiling
dances the girl upstairs

"Homecoming's next week
we'll have to make your mum"

                              turning down Monette
                              car and truck oncoming

                              parting traffic
                              bounding to disembark

                              with Edgar Allan Poe
                                      —outside the gym

"I don't need to do that"
"You had one last year?"

"Yeah, Anna made it."
"We could make you one.

You wore it, right?"
"Yeah, but I don't need one."

                              scofflaw and squander
                              time again

                              wife           —gone
                              girls in Aggieland

                              scofflaw and squander
                              time again

# Ibn Zaydún to Wallada

It's not just the physical.
I love that though.
It's the intimate talking too.
Yes, we have it,
but it is not the same.

There is the tension,
but it will always be unfulfilled
and there is the sorrow
as if two barbed wire fences
have been erected between us

with ten feet between and our touch
now touchless. It is death while living.

## Invocation (for Barbra Riley)

O daughters of Thunderbolt & Language Memory
Your wooded wonders saturated periphery—
                                    News obliterate

*En plein aire, caméra nature morte*—maelstrom
Landscape of heath health—Polyhymnia belief
                                    Hear our plea

Montage photo silver leaf
Moss stone grave site double steps
                                    In Tennessee

Erato, Giotto, polluted Clio—deep state
Mount Helicon, Terpsichore dithyrambic
                                    Urania freight

Thalia darling, Crystal Method, Calliope
Frost weed muses, bunny badger deer
                                   Hesiod surreal tree

Euterpe laurel wreath pillow talk—cardinal fawn
Melpomene cactus death mask, longhorn chaos
                                  Eden cabin trait

O Henry David journal thunderstorm
Paint your mullein Walden Holler Creek
                                  Birds—talk to me

Built newness—discovered time
Natural pigment process, UV black and white
                    Forty-watt caliphate


Rooster coffee everywhere morning bedroom sound
Direction Zephyr to syzygy, same time absurdity—shutter
                                                  Photo apogee

# Thinking of You, Robb Jackson

Old moon hangs cold light that dazzles waves on
Corpus Bay as you, Robb, saw light upon Lake Erie
as you roamed her shores through nights and days.

That suitcase full of your father's ties. "Vintage,"
you said, "Worth something to someone." Rebuffed by
wardrobe of 501s, flannel shirts and jean jacket.

The colors and designs as you sifted through
silk fabric, quality sown, fifty or more to string up
a man.                                          Robb,

you warned me.
Those "turkeys, they don't care" will whittle you to nothing.
That I was only a "lettuce picker" in their eyes and ledger.

You warned me.
Take the road bearing left before crossing the bridge
on the left, you'll see the Pecos & Rio Grande confluence.

Raptors soar off the bridge on thermals.
The sheep you mentioned were there on the far bank.
Both warnings understood, valuable.

Soon when I walk through the weeping juniper on mountain loam
in the Chisos Basin, starlight illuminating Casa Grande and
Emory Peak, waiting for a bobcat to pad by on prowl for a pocket mouse.

Thinking of you, Robb Jackson, as I "shooby doo" this "word vomit," witnessing the last quarter moon rise past midnight on Thanksgiving. Coldness seeps into aching bones propped up but for how long?

## **Pairs, Thrice** *(Muwashshaha)*

Traces she left on the pillow
Mark her sleep after bliss
When she unfolded a blanket
In one fluid motion, letting it float
To the turf, ironing out the billows
Before unpacking a meal to enjoy

    My love's dexterity and grace, viewed—
    Ice skating, caved my chest
    — Continuous throbs to this day

Pomes! —shapes and sculpts—
A shower quenches thought
With pelting droplets
Cascading down face
To your breasts
That I long to kiss

    Heat restored, feeling felt in limbs
    As spring begets buds to bloom
    Renewal blazes forth though throbs

Over and over lapis beads jangle
Nipples redden and heat rises
Wetness floods and your longing
Inanna, becomes too much
To be patient with Dumuzi's cedar

Rising to plow your vulva

        Bust of eternal rest looms closer
        Too many meds, not enough exercise
        — Burst of energy come forth

Till! Settle into my waxing climax.
Ibn Zaydun reciprocate and slides
Between Wallada's unfolding golden
thighs with tongue to her clitoris,
until sheet grasp ready to explode
As fingers dips and agitates

        Four fingers on a hand
        The color of your roses
        The garden's cynosure

To rub your Gräfenberg
Vulcan fingers deeply nadir
Wallada breathing the breath
The moan—the leg clenching
Scissor thigh and guttural
Animal O O O al Andalus!

        Rosemary, lavender, gardenias and pelargoniums
        Lemon and orange heated summer buds
        Night gardens of paradise

# My Whisper

My whisper winds on a breeze,

traces your neck,

loosens your hair,

billows and ruffles

                your skirt.

My whisper glints like dawn

over my shoulder.

Your face completely lit,

ravishes and radiant,

                your smile.

## Death Stairs (For Pam Brouillard)

Death Stairs at Dalkeith House.
Stone turnpike stairs.
Servants rotating up or down
for royalty and now we walk

worn and wobbly pavers
jutting from an axis pole
cold to the soles, WC on
another level—take the

Death Stairs for the morning pee,
to shower, brush your teeth.
Drams of fine Oban scotch
strong ale. That hand rail

semidetached on one level,
the next only loose hung rope
teeter on up or nearly fall
down, the haunted Death Stairs.

A cavalier apparition cold
passes through your heart—
another dram for strength
—before talkin' Dalkeith House's

Death Stairs. At the bottom
were found a shiny pair

of black Wellies—nobody
claims to place them there.

Wellington's boots came off his
marble statue near the Tartan Stairs.
Transformed into black rubber boots
to go up and down all night on

the Death Stairs. Take your life
in your hands each flight.
Sober or not—the cold penetrates all
each turnpike step of the Death Stairs.

# On Each Other's Birthday

My paternal grandparents
died on each other's birthday.

He going first, September 30th.
She next, February 24th.

78 and 79, respectively. Even listed
following each other, in an online database

though they'd been divorced
for fifty-four years

and only married for two.
Six years after their burials

I married and on the honeymoon,
caravaning through Europa, tent-camping

with bride outside Assisi's walls. It was all
quite a shock of info that honeymoon day.

The queen mum's smiling avec silly hat,
the relic cloth of Clare's basilica,

Francis gave up all his silk pantaloons.
Then viewing Giotto's realistic frescoes—

Saint Francis of Assisi receiving stigmata.
The queen mum's 90-year broad beam.

My grandmother was Clara.
My grandfather was Francis.

In Alameda, the island where they died, she never
stopped, nor slowed her Oldsmobile Cutlass

as he walked to open the church doors;
too afraid of his anger and trigger finger.

They weren't meant to exist
together in this realm, however,

if he hadn't dropped his pantaloons
and she acquiesced, I wouldn't be here.

# The Divisionist

> "*You see control can never be a means to any practical end. ... It can never be a means to anything but more control. ... Like junk...*" The Divisionists occupy a mid-way position, could in fact be termed moderates. ... They are called Divisionist because they literally divide (William S. Burroughs *Naked Lunch*, 164).

I see your skanky party line MAGA hats – pantsuit votes

no thought bypassing control to utter chaos


flipping through your Facebook control buttons

under your late capitalism thumb of buy buy buy


Divisionist do not sell your name and numbers

for anything but the hard cash and credit


you're just another unit on their silicone abacus

Bitcoins sluiced in Jami Khashoggi severed limbs from


spilled blood when Facebook and Amazon divide us

from our time we're forced to spend on the atomic clock


ticking dirty bombs of bupkis delight cooked to feast upon

on the other sides of walls of wankers—orange has lost its ap-


peal! Divisionist the douche of *Professor Fingerbottom*'s

experimentations of sexual replicants and rhetorical fear


the cyborg's *sucking emptiness* moving from cell to cell

as the human virus slouches off like a rough beast.

*Professor Fingerbottom* "I studied neurology under Professor Fingerbottom in Vienna" (William S. Burroughs *Naked Lunch* 165).

*Sucking emptiness* "D.B.—Definitive Bulletin: "The Sender will be defined by negatives. A low pressure area, a sucking emptiness" (William S. Burroughs *Naked Lunch* 168).

# Chupacabra and Welder Mask Man

Chupacabra was sucking goat blood
in the early morning light when
Welder Mask Man saw the fangs
dig deeper into the white neck
and the ruby blood dribbled down
its bleating throat. Welder Mask

Man sat and watched with intrigue
how Chupacabra's fangs sunk
into the jugular, not minding the
frantic hooves kick-out. Both were
patient for the blood to drain from
the wide-eyed goat whose legs

shat upon were losing life fast.
Chupacabra saw Welder Mask
Man, and sank its fangs, if
possible, deeper once again.
Their eyes in contact, a connection,
a pact of sorts was communicated

that Welder Mask Man waited for
Chupacabra to finish with his
goat sucking and then Welder
Mask Man would take goat from
Chupacabra for his own, to put on
a spit and roast it over his hot coals.

# After the Hurricane

Saws rent the air two days before Harvey came.
The line for Plylox was more than a hundred people long.
After boarding up the windows and sandbagging the doors

we left early the day before landfall
to San Antonio. Carol took us in
with our daughter plus five cats

till Harvey blew over—two days later
we came back to blown-out signs.
We were lucky—minor damage.

Lattice on the balcony blew off
two links of fencing came down.
Fixed them up right away.

Some were not as lucky.
Chainsaws buzzed at all hours.
We kept thanking our fortune

quietly because we knew
Rockport and Port A
were nearly wiped off the map.

Took down all the boards, sawed up downed limbs.
Threw out all the food in the fridge and freezer.
Power out for a few days—what a near miss.

Voices met said otherwise: "Six feet
Of water in the house," "We lost all our
Trees," "We lost our condo in Rockport."

"I was stranded—My uncle came for me
in an airboat—swarms of ants everywhere—
took me to my parents—then we all

got into a bay boat and drove over—
seven feet of water down the freeway."
We're lucky to be here now.

## Her Crossed Legs Show

                        Her crossed legs show.
Her short skirt rides up her thighs on the bench.
Eyes dart toward her left and front in search

                        of whom she planned to meet.
She pulls at the hem, adjusts her collar strap
turning her head away, her hair swings an arc

                        of gold through the thick heated air.
Her wrist jangles as she flicks open a fan;
commences to cool her nervousness.

# Written Robes
*(following Wallada bint al-Mustakfi)*

(down right side)

Stellar grace and fire provide life


(across right side)

Anarchy amplifies all expression

# The Mathematics of the Last Act (for Dorothea Rockburne)

Peyton Farquhar sways
a pattern marked by his urine
drops upon Owl Creek after his

erection recedes, the ejaculated
semen, the last shots aimed for his wife.
Too viscous to contribute, swimming,
squirming, on tailored breaches, a curve
flow slows down, melding, attaching
corpus with clothe, epidermis with
Haploid cells, wither away by a Yankee ploy.

The circles in the current spread downstream,
semi-soft chunks plunge deeper where
trout swim forth to nibble-taste
along the declivity of the directrix,
a plantation owner, whip cracker,
Tea bagger, toxic farmer; deer hunter's last
defecation creates a watershed dead zone.

# **Obituary** *(Muwashshaha)*

In this God-forsaken Bible
rust Belt, Margaret Screws
lived 98 years before going
to the Lord on November 19th
2016 at Mount Carmel CC.

    A dedicated nurse, who
    learned her asses and lube trade
    in the same hospital where she was born,
    St. Paul's in Big D
    as Margaret Ann Thurmon.

Moved to Kermit with her friend Janie
to nurse that West Texas big sky
at Robinson McClure Hospital
where she gave a shot of penicillin
to her love, George Dewey "Pete" Screws.

    Humble Margaret screws
    Pete's Fitz-Willie and pops
    out eight children before
    Sun Oil Company shipped them
    to San Isidro Sun Oil Field.

A school nurse, then a quick in 'n out.
The *Kingsville Record*'s headline
"Margaret Screws Bishop

now Screws in Premont."
Nurse of Brock County, humble, butt-proud.

> Oh, Saint Teresa of the Infant Flower Catholic church of Premont!
> How do we know Margaret Screws?
> The eight kids' 19 grandchildren
> their 39 great-grandchildren
> and their 3 great-great-grandchildren.

Her boys weren't all that proud or humble.
After childhood torment, teasing and torture
two of the sons changed their name to Crews.
The five girls all married, thus taking their husbands' name.
except for David Screws in Stephenville.

> Remember, when you're pressing the button
> while you're lying in that hospital bed,
> mainlining meds and saline solution,
> plus filling up that colostomy bag,
> remember, "Oh nurse?" Margaret Screws.

# Sallipraxius

"What is this idea here?"
She wanted him to unpack his thoughts,

pick them over and burn those that were
in her mind abhorrent.

She pointed to the words he had typed.
"Do you even know what you're saying?" Silence.

"You need to unpack these thoughts
that are stacked upon themselves."

"What good will that do? I feel safer
having the lone key to the whole kit

and caboodle." She looked at him,
knowing he was paranoid. She was paranoid

too, though she had substantiated she couldn't be
paranoid. She had written a book to prove that.

# Update

He was texting Godot
to see if he was

                      moving chairs
                      hanging out with the rhinos
                      on the balcony with Genet

                      listening to Krapps Last Tape
                      having a pint with Murphy
                      watching Malone have sex with Moll

                      hiding in Mr. Knott's closet
                      reading the movement of lips
                      buried in the sand

there was no answer
there was no phone

## 7 18 16  *(Muwashshaha)*

Racist and richest
triumphant Trumpt.
Wives video their husbands
shot by cops,
bleeding to death.
Rainbow dipping dots.

        Claustrophobic gun
        metal muzzle meltdown.
        The NRA constellation:
        Orlando,

Falcon Heights,
Baton Rouge,
Dallas again.
Jack-booted thugs,
"Open carry" and "Don't

        Tread on me" unfurled
        like yesterday
        at the DQ complex
        in Picacho, AZ

where knives sold.
And that gaunt beat man
holding a gleaming new hatchet
said, "They won't mess with me

now." A tasty glint

>   in his eyes,
>   hunting each other,
>   old Sport,
>   for the Richest

and the Racist.
Control, the screws
tighten their observations
across the grid.
Why we need martial law with
Fear and Fear itself

>   smiles with bloody hands
>   spreads, showers xenophobia
>   like growth hormones
>   to chickens in a hothouse.

Warps our sensibilities.
Bulks up our hate.
Ramps up our anger.
Feeds us semi-automatic
conversion bump stocks,
bullets and blood.

>   Kill Kill Kill Kill!
>   Their Trumpt stocks rise
>   before the market bottoms out

and the military steps onto your street.

A planet of apes,
with an apology to our brethren beasts
for such demeaning comparison.
It would be better for this country
rather than costume and farkle
to walk into the desert and disappear.

Shovel now the gutted
carved up maps
of civilization's arts,
ashes from the crematory that will
flutter from the transcontinental
trucks ~~cocks and cunts~~ I don't want

        to speak these words.
        A realization
        that murder
        an onion layer

peeling back to Maslow's
Safety when all should Actualize.
To get from S to A
breathe deeply   — exhale.
again, breathe
                — exhale.

        Naked

as the day you were born

repeat after me —

"How can I help?"

# Ofay

My hips don't lie
Honkeys still want to control your existence
I rather be Man Ray or gay but I'm just Ofay.

[[Don't call me nigger, whitey (sample of Sly & the Family Stone)]]

Drop the towers to tell me to buy
Want women to admit to their boss they love *jouissance*
I rather be East Bay Ray or a Steller's Jay but I'm just Ofay

[[John Wayne was a Nazi / He liked to play SS (sample of MDC)]]

Raise a border fence, lower regulatory EPA
Frack the frigging landscape to pollute the aquifers
I rather have died in My Lai but I'm just Ofay

[[When I see John I'm ashamed to be white (sample of MDC)]]

Squeeze our enemy's banking nuts each day
Send the Seals to secure another KFC
I rather get high and play the blues but I'm just Ofay

[[Don't call me nigger, whitey (sample of Sly & the Family Stone)]]

Heat the Keystone XL pipes—cash for landscape chaos
Privatize the rubber finger up your ass
I rather not pray any day and I'm still just Ofay

## Song Poem Wha be Wha

Put on my riding jams
bop bop ba

Put on my riding jams
bop bop
                ba

everybody understands
todo el mundo
ScRAM

napo slapo
wind's pickn' up
everybody's special
like you

enough
to make some casxh

heh he hun hun shun
simultaneously double both
snap

I'm Zora's
unfettered
pulled hamstring
and all

but it's gonna take much more than me
to bring some
                          Pax

do do a do du

Please
reach out

drop your guns

and get killed

with me


the planet
        is getting ready to explode

and all us old punks
too fat
lost our doc martins'
                boots steel toe

there ain't nothing
but too loose
by constriction

I once dreamed of buying a vintage toaster
but it blew up the house

nothing in this world is worth losing
'cept the plastic bags

zuppa Pacifica

brutality


water
going down in flames

# Chaos!

More than a theory
Siegfried versus Max
like the Clash
Get out of Control

Chaos!

99 in a tight dress
her sultry words
beckon childhood lust
embrace unrequited love

Chaos!

Today's photobombs
plethora of violence
switching, punching & executions
Neeli Cherkovski, Bob Kaufman's dead

Chaos!

An NFL auto de fé
NSA station in CCA
"Stukas over Bedrock"
Drones over Padre

Chaos!

Bleeding eye death Africa

Chaos!

Invasion tanks & rocket launchers

Chaos!

Death water bubonic air

Chaos!

XO! XO! X!
Oh no, no control
mere anarchy!
Chaos!

# Protest Infinity Pantoum (for Dorothy Alexander)

Airborne, uproar, buzz
Violent jackboot cadence feet
Who beats you against the concrete
Five-O, [clap] PoPo, [clap] Fuzz

Violent jackboot cadence feet
Confer sling-jack and truncheon
Take out trees and fell women
Who beats you against the concrete

Confer sling-jack and truncheon
Pepper spray, water cannon
Attack dogs, big mouth Bannon
Take out trees and fell women

Pepper spray, water cannon
Toilet bowl tweets from the chump
Racist prattle, Seig Heil Trump
Attack dogs, big mouth Bannon

Toilet bowl tweets from the chump
Puxxy grab, #metoo
Abuser, predator, coup
Racist prattle, Seig Heil Trump

Puxxy grab, #metoo
Cocktail hour, Molotov

Street marches, howl, "Fuck off"
Abuser, predator, coup

Cocktail hour, Molotov
Airborne, uproar, buzz
Five-O, [stomp] PoPo, [stomp] Fuzz
Street marches, howl, "Fuck off"

# West Texas Desert Bloom

West Texas desert bloom
Fireballs and white panel van

Of security details follows, plates
Unknown, toss down cervezas

Smoke a bowl to exorcise the doom
Peel back the petals to Los Alamos' Burning Man

Pecos giant donut tumbled down a well
Acrid smoke billows out the cavern cracks

Fried sands a bank of glass
Gun blasts erases anyone caught on tape

No longer alive, but truly Milton's Hell
Aquifer ditty, no gas, light a match—bloom

## You Tender Hogs

You tender hogs
rip the world into shreds

speed the process of disintegration
challenge the good

in the petty
disgusting

simplicity of selfishness.
Tired and aching

in weakness
nearly impossible

to decipher
the geometry of your egotism—

everything is clotted
a disgusting network

in the last stages of fractures
still incomprehensible shape and form

perched on the edge—it falls
into nothingness rot

soft unprotected
membranes dying

bloody fingers
take your food

orange bells rung
broke your code.

He said, "You remind me
of my 3rd husband."

She said, "You remind me
of my first cadaver

half in the bag
and cold to the touch."

# Hand Written Language Analysis

Punk started before that dictatrix Thatcher.
Kaous for Chaos.

The curve portion of d in "down" split form read "clown."
Her "all" was written in such a way to read as "911."

Surviving the second and third purge of intellectuals.
Riven words towards graphemes broken on the wheel.

The difference between trot and trout is u.
Fill the casket with blue books.

Out running the meat wagon
into Jay Gould's gold supply.

The hunchback albino dwarf—
look out for Grendel!

A straight line bores a crooked path,
Roughly preserving Joe Adame in drag.

Twisted pigments blind the sensibilities.
The late-night street light with the bald eagle perched.

Double blind money pit two blocks from the bay.
Sip and surf—*eguzki* naked on the beach.

# I Am Werg

I am Werg, my name comes from you.
That is, you make me swell with sap,
ripe with wild dancing and debauch.

An excess of your ambrosia vessel.
The urn curves for the harpoon;
succulent impalement in this lap.

Gyrations and undulations abound.
Lips-locked, fat tongue balls; release.
Handgrip maximus, now suck festoon,

pulsation, urn's internal clench.
Moan to thrust, bellow and ball,
clasp arms adorn the neck of the beast.

Ground flesh welding flesh with heat and juice.
Claws nap hair tight; pulls head back to bare neck;
skin-licks an utterance signals the orgasmic call.

## Still Life

She loves to wrap her Benghazi arms around his waist,
squeeze his two smart-bombs in her palm. Lick

his ISIL until he explodes over Sykes-Picot Pact.
Makes him devour her 28 Mordad until he says,

"I cannot breathe," and chokes him until she fills
his Gaza strip with her urine and her ruddy

secretion. It was in that Weather Top-Six Gallery
Nexus of Roctober, she passes lead through his skull.

# Then Again, On the Road
(two steps from losing it)

Not the happy-go-lucky fool,
they pop up like tombstones
beyond the lichgate
straight from Old English.
The horrors of a life

after the last family generation
convulsed on the floor after croaking,
"I love you."
The shambles continue to exude like blood sweat
a mixture of Burke's two sublimes.
Terror may be winning.

There is an exit at the back of this room.
It's just a quiet pop.
Who knows what's on the other side
though the stairs, if they're even there,
lead downward
to the deepest circles of Alighieri inferno.

I'll just sight-see
If nobody minds too much.
Just show me where you placed
The colonel.

# Warp and Woof

*si mi voz muriera en tierra*        *if my voice dies on land*
*llevadla al nivel del mar*            *take it to sea level*
*y dejadla en la ribera*              *and leave it on the shore*
                     *Rafael Alberti*

*heart-broken shark's teeth rattle with grief in the belfry*
                *Jean Arp (translated by G P Skratz)*

## Part I

Gulf Sunrise          —          like mercury
     leaving the larger glob with a waver
Blue Heron perched upon the dunes
        Beak faces the spread of light

Across the warp and woof
      That weaves wet sand
           to dune undulations

            In contact
Garbage bag and garden gloves

          Kneel and squat
Root out washed-up trash
      plastic in any form
Like a pig snuffling for truffles

The sea expanse
        ripples to roar
North South
        The beach line open

                        Cool salt tang on the tongue
Recognizes the rubbish
Cigarette butts
        Soaked diapers
                  Both shoved into wind blown
                      Three-ply
                            — inland view

Foredunes of blown sand
        under a mantle
              dropseed & sea oats

the tangle of railroad vine
                and gulf croton
        on the ridge, forbs
     purple morning glories flutter
                  as ragged warp or broken fill

Foot sluggish step towards the heights
Slowed to watch the unsymmetrical v —
        Seventeen gliding brown pelicans — low
                    over thundering surf

Kitbag toss of cutlery,

        Sand-stuffed Yoplait knocked
        Free and falls into piles of time

Always working up the dune to the ridge
                To see the inner island
    Found solace
                    Cleaning this beach

Ridge-top view—bright panorama of the 4x4s
Lined like a funeral procession at this punctual
                    pulverization of the Big Shell Beach—Lichgate
                        The plum cemetery, Oceanic
                            Watery grave

Leave all behind, step down into the folds
    Of wayward dunes splattered athwart
        Red & yellow petals of Indian Blanket

                Relief was sought
    Coffee, water and jumbled ride
    Smoke off urine rose during survey
        Dante's cut Bolgia came to mind
            *the fish are shimmering over the horizon*[1]

                  Then appeared — the shark
    Swimming the air with strong tail kick
        High overhead as if forty yards out

---

[1] Line 113, Canto XI *The Divine Comedy: Inferno* by Dante Alighieri. The Sixth Circle of Heretics. "che i Pesci guizzan su per l' orizzonta."

                                                            Deep in the cut

Immediately knew, *deluded*            as it swam closer

I began to speak out loud when it addressed me
                        "What is your name, O frightened one?"
Without hesitation or pause, I said,
                        "I'm Hallucinating Thomas."

"Though that's not your name, but close enough to receive
                our greeting. Do you recognize me?"
        Switchtail closer
                To circle three meters away


        Nervous, though not scarred, thought


                                        *Whiskers*

                                                *Fu Manchu*
"You have swum far, Nurse Shark, from your lurking post
        at Sombrero Reef off the Keys. Are there many of you
        here?"


        "*Uukanipo* – two great sharks – twin brothers
Received your message and plea on Malaquite
        Like Gemini sharks – Caster and Pollux

                Sunless, Scorpio viewed
                        Antares and Mars. You
                        named her nipples

      Ripe and twinkling"

            — I'm disturbed
    I'm not sure which is more disconcerting
  Speaking shark or swimming air
           How will I reckon
     With friends, whose whole beings
         Question this moment now?

        "*Kaaipai* is near,
Hallucinating Thomas. In the parlance of our times, this is your cross
  to bear."
"Sometimes the Bear eats you, *strikes and gutters*[2],
       that dawn was not
         a simple *ritardando*."


"Hallucinating Thomas,
  you flounder-pluck the sand
    thought better to avoid the gut.
  Why have you not swum the hole?"
"I'm not ready for that abyss."
    "Ready or not, you must enter now."
"Where will it take me?"

     "Below the hill of the Whale
       *Pu' u Kohalā*
     Past the sitting stone
        *Mailekini*

---

[2] *The Big Lebowski*. Dir. J. Coen & E. Coen. 1997.

                    And into the brine
To the temple      of Sharks

                                      *Hale o Kapuni heiau*"

"The Big Island, Hawai'i?"
"Yes.                I am *Aumakua*,
            Semi-diós as the *Slinger*" [3]

                      "— Specter
of the unreal,
    *arena te quiero como el tiempo*"

        "You see me,
                Hallucinating Thomas,
                            Yes."

"Yes, as clear
        As Indian Blanket billows
                This fabrication
The fabric of life
        Woven crosswise –

Stripped of human influence
        The surge of wave and wind
                Fluctuates in these surroundings
                        Dismantles and deteriorates
                                Dunes thatched by vine and root"

---

[3] *Slinger* or *Gunslinger* by Edward Dorn

"Come, Hallucinating Thomas.

        I will show you

                The gut —

Come."
## Part II

*I do not know the old language* [4]
Refinery fires inland                  sfumato Horizon
Purls the Nueces shore
       A multitude of Barad-dûr
            Belches sulfur dioxide
                 In the *Cities of Red Night* [5]

Tri-blade props
      Cutting flyway swathes
           An army of aves Molochs

In the archipelago of air
      What brooding coil awaits
          *Coup de main*
              The inevitable day

In this cut *Aumakua* leads.

Luck has been with us that we may dance with our loves
Instead of fighting for life, as so many do, a daily occurrence

---

[4] Line 13, "The Fire Passages 13" *Bending the Bow* by Robert Duncan.

[5] *City of Red Nights* a novel by William S. Burroughs.

We empathize with those willing to strap on explosives to see their god
We can only feel remorse for those that lead them down this blind alley

A path they believe paved with gold and honor
Only awash with blood of their sisters and brothers

## Part III

Garbage, firmly clutched
        Each step measured
                By loss

Through verdure
        Gulf dune paspalum and bitter panicum
        Around knoll and hummock

*Aumakua* glides with kicktail
        the nurse shark looks back
                *coup d'œil* with its dead eyes

"Hallucinating Thomas, we are near.
        Exigence is upon us"
                Its Shark words fade around the bend

Pluck a semi-immersed water bottle
        An addition to the plastic baggage
                Clearing the sand bar

Level with moi – Sky buoys
    The sharks circled and bobbed
        two fathoms up
            over a blood-splattered dais

Four of the compass
    Await their lead or do I run
        *It's long way to the 4x4s*
        *Aumakua* spoke—


    "Hallucinating Thomas,
  Come down here to the breach."

    "My heart's not for such intense surroundings."
  "You don't lie very well, do you, Hallucinating one?" Spoke the Great White
"I've watched you over the years, here along these cuts, like the ones
    On the palms of your hands

    Some shallower while other deeper and lengthier
    —even with a hole of rotting flesh
you remember plucking that white putrid knob of flesh
    from your inner palm."

*The stink of rot*
"You're here for renewal, Hallucinating Thomas"
        The Great White's monocular eye bobbed
    "Does that mean you stamp my hand?"

"In some sense, yes, stamping will happen," A Mako spoke.
"Though not as you may think," said the other Mako.
                      Nurse Shark spoke, "Come down to the breach."

The sybarites' call invokes a tune
            Commence Pavlovian froth for that "foul ecstasy."
Experiment with shapes, colors, tense and vectors
    Taster of oyster pools
        Horseradish root-ground
    The color of ivory and bloody cocktail
    Sauce on the palate for the tongue
    Tip to lick
        Up and around
                That carrot plunge


    The breach was a wide almond gap
    Fizzing water boiled like old Morning Glory
Blue yellow and a sulfur stench unites
putresce
    mold and rust
        —blood splattered

    edges skirt languish grasses among maggoty limbs

The breaker far away, like an artillery shot in the distance
Cadence metronomic – though palladiumless

Upon closer viewing,
        just above the breach of faith

                    was a nearly invisible catwalk

silver timbers smeared
                with bile, blood and excrement.

        "Who sawed these planks from tree trunks?
        Where are the baskets of air?"
"Careful where you step, Hallucinating Thomas
                                                We're hungry,"
                                Spoke *Uukanipo* in unison.


A brown Pelican flew low
        Buzzed and bellowed,


        "Flies and fleas
Sichden Kopfzer brechen -- with broke teeth and heads." [6]


            In formation, other pelicans glide—speaking
In chorus
                    "Send abundant
Protection. Here are the used and weathered condoms
Sand crusted,
                forced to wear
                        sliding up the shaft
                    though limp as a Romani
                        in the gas chamber
                                waiting for a shower."

---

[6] Hans (Jean) Arp poem

"Fly off, beaks! Before we mince your squawking feathers"
*Aumakua* gnashed her jaws with a snap

## Part IV

"I am *Kaaipai*"
    The deep voiced Great White spoke
        "We were breeding
                in the cold brine

        waiting for backpack scouts
                to tempt the Pacific

        as you held the beaker
                of white gas – lit

        at night on Wild Cat beach
                like the mad bomber [7]

        cocking your arm, tossing lit beaker
                flame soared and dripped

        into your hair that caught fire –
                that beacon beckoned

        kick tailed to a closer gut near shore
                awaiting you to run to surf, to us

---

[7] Mad bomber was a nickname for Oakland Raiders quarterback Daryle Lamonica

        to extinguish the flames dancing upon your head
            the Leonard threw you down to grainy sand

        he rolled you till your head smoked fused stinking strands
            we gnashed in the gut, missing our moment of
            your blood

—stop on these planks           to rise again"

"*Uukanipo*'s hunger — great indeed
    Pucela, Pucela," *Uukanipo* invoked.

Each step creaks towards the breach. I spoke,
"What sea is clearer than the pomegranate body
        holding the flame?"[8]   —*Aumakua* swished.
    "Pucela, Pucela," Pollux and Caster duet

"Stop and rot, Hallucinating Thomas, in our mouths and guts.
    Feel the sedulous scythe
    Limb by limb
        Speak out the crime
Flesh ripped
        Bones crushed
        Blood bursts
        All to rise
            Now lean back
                This won't hurt too much."

---

[8] Lines 212-3 Canto LXXIX *The Cantos*. Ezra Pound

      Boiling water below the slick boards
             Feet in the air
          Stretched out

"Speak out the crimes.
        You know which they are."
                "I stole booze and resold it."
Brother Pollux *Uukanipo* tore off my right arm.
                Pain was immense
                "I spread diseases never
                    telling others."
Brother Caster *Uukanipo* snapped my left arm off.
                Blood spurted out
                each socket.
                "I coveted her
                body with relish."
Aumakua bit my upper left thigh
      Tugged twice and powered her teeth
      Clean through the femur.
                Nearly blacked
                out I screamed,
                "I believe in noth-
                ing but energy."
The Great White *Kaaipai* crunched my final limb.
                In agony, life
                spilling out
                The sharks began
                to masticate
                Nosh and nip

Gorge and gulp
Till my head
entered *Kaaipai*
His razor teeth
pierced my chest
    Echoed,
    in that
    wet
    lodge
    a final yelp.

# You Want to Bring Your Guns to My Class

You want to bring your guns to my class?
Texas law says it's all right to play John Wayne.
Well—                you can kiss my ass.

Already in the cross hairs of educational heehaw,
Weaving regulatory blather of Chancellor Inane.
Who wants to bring their guns to my class?

The 2nd amendment's real concern is militia, there's the flaw.
Hey doctor with the ankle holster, you're a scatterbrain!
Here's some praxis, kiss my ass!

Pearl handle in her backpack, I spit out my coleslaw.
Jesus! Jenny! This doesn't happen in Spain!
Where they don't allow guns in any class.

If you want to bring your Glock 26 or 43, withdraw.
Go gun free; be brave, smart and humane.
Don't come to campus to shoot anyone's ass.

What about my rights! Ya'll say it's the damn law!
Exploring the mind and universe is ours to ascertain.
You're in danger bringing your guns to my class.
When the OK Corral breaks out, I'll be yelling, "Kiss My ASS!"

# Moon Earth Eros Sun

Moon Earth Eros Sun.
                       The knee bent or squat exercise,
another stone in hand, some rough grit others sharp
like the obsidian found. Now kept on office bookshelf;

its translucent edges never chipped. Below Ferrin Knob,
old Appalachia trail bones culled.
                          Brother Alan's rock,
a large hunk smoothed, had always already forty years

plus. Together, hiking Ute Trail, Alpine to Milner Pass,
we found that stone load.        Frederick Douglass's home
on hilltop, three white stones winnowed;
                      *Ogbanje iyi-uwa.*

Chert from Monkton Down, divided gift, roundabout
tumuli walk to the sarsen stone circles of Avebury.
Climbed granite,
              Half Dome, Banner Peak boulder hop.

Water smoothed rounds plucked from Colorado River
mud below the desert varnish rust walls of the
Moab furnace.
             Delicate Arch, a stone throw away.

Lava Pele threw skyward. A need to behold and beholden
stardust particles.

In every negotiated space are unpocketed found stones for luck, for safety, for memory, for love.

# Fall

Golden rod, burnt orange and firebrand red

flutter bunches sail through the canopy like spinnakers

to an array of paths that skirt smoke mountains

to the narrow roads that carve the Blue Ridge

to the still lake bottoms' depths full of compact varve,

carpeting the forest floors.


Golden rod, burnt orange and firebrand red

cover battlefields of dead and forgotten warriors from the Iroquois to the Algonquin

from the whipped slaves running for their lives following the north mossy tree side to the pine cone burning raid on Harpers Ferry

from the graves of Tom Wolfe in Asheville and Lowell's Kerouac to the tombs of Confederate and Union alike in their scatterings of pitched fights to drawn-out battles and charges

from the black lung coal miners, the meth labs hidden on hill sides, the alcohol-fueled car accidents on blind turns

from the French Broad, the Susquehanna, the Rappahannock, the
Shenandoah, the Merrimac and the Kennebec.


Golden rod, burnt orange and firebrand red

colors of spring's death mask all with vibrant hues stolen from dawn and sunset

that wait to be blanketed by a dusting of snow, falling through the bare grey
skeleton branches of Appalachia.

www.ingramcontent.com/pod-product-compliance
Lightning Source LLC
Chambersburg PA
CBHW031108080526
44587CB00011B/886